STRANGE FACE

Adventures with a lost
Nick Drake recording

Michael Burdett

empreinte
cordiale

First published by Empreinte Cordiale 2013
This edition published 2015

ISBN: 978-0-9576246-1-0

Copyright © Michael Burdett 2013

Michael Burdett has asserted his right under the Copyright, Designs and Patents Act 1988 to be identified as the author of this work.

All Rights Reserved. No part of this publication may be reproduced in any form or by any means without the written permission of the publishers.

Cover design by Grainger & Wolff

Text typeset by Shore Books, Blackborough End, Norfolk.

Printed and bound in the United Kingdom.

Contents

From Skip to Strange Face	vii
About Nick Drake	xiii
Photos and Stories	1
About Michael Burdett	265
Acknowledgements	266

To Claire, who patiently lived with and listened to every word, and then corrected most of them.

And to Jeannie B.

with love xx

From Skip to Strange Face

In the late 1970s, I was working as a post boy at Island Records. One summer's afternoon I was asked to give a hand taking a huge pile of tapes out to a skip at the back of the building in British Grove, Chiswick. These were spools of quarter-inch tape and boxes of cassettes – demo tapes, old copies and recordings that weren't required anymore.

I helped take the piles of tapes out to the skip, which was already half full of the sort of stuff that record companies regularly used to throw out. As I worked, I thought that some of the bigger spools would be useful to me in the studio that I was starting to put together. There were also some cassettes and tapes by bands I liked.

I went to see my boss and asked if it would be alright if I could keep some of the tapes and take them home. He replied that I was welcome to help myself to anything that was in the skip.

In the evening after work I completely emptied that skip. Mainly, I was looking for large quarter-inch tapes, especially ones that had no edits or leader tape between the tracks, because I could re-use them. I remember that there were old tapes by Traffic and Andy Fraser of Free, which I took home and taped over.

Right at the bottom of the pile were a couple of tapes that grabbed my attention. One was a demo cassette by a friend's band. I took it with the intention of showing him what had happened to his beloved work (though in the end it felt too cruel). The other was a scruffy little five-inch spool of quarter-inch Emitape. Written on the orange box in black felt tip pen were the words 'Cello Song…Nick Drake 7.5ips mono copy …With love xx'.

I looked at the box and was close to leaving it, but it was the phrase 'With Love' that stopped me. I thought, that has to be Nick Drake's handwriting. And it was simply this belief that made me pick it up.

Drake had been dead for about five years. I had never met him but

I knew his material well and liked it.

I took the little orange box home, along with a huge armful of tapes and cassettes, because I simply could not let it go to the dump.

I have always been a bit of a hoarder – I still have my cub uniform, for crying out loud – and for a long while I didn't play the tape. It went into storage and eventually moved around the country with me.

After leaving Island Records, I had a career as an A&R man before doing a bit of record production and engineering, and eventually ended up writing music for television, which is what I still do to this day.

In 1999, I moved to mid-Wales to take a bit of a break from television composition and to record an album myself. I had a studio installed in a beautiful cottage on the bank of a powerful little river and wrote and recorded a dozen tracks there.

During the composition period, one of the tracks gave me quite a few problems. It was a piece written for three pianos and I had a lot of trouble finishing it. I acted as every miserable composer does and busied myself with all kinds of distractions, including setting up an old Revox tape recorder and going through loads of quarter-inch tapes that I had accumulated over the years. It was interesting and fun, but most of all, it was perfect displacement activity.

Over twenty years after retrieving it from the skip, for the first time I took the Nick Drake tape out of its box and threaded it on to the machine. I settled back in a huge armchair with the sound of the river coming in through the open window, and relaxed.

The track started. I thought something was wrong with the tape machine. The guitar sounded different. And then two cellos came in. They played a flourish I didn't recognise. This wasn't the version I was used to. This wasn't Cello Song from Five Leaves Left. The percussion started and was much busier. It felt…well…funkier. And finally Drake's voice came in, beautifully recorded but different, ever so slightly different. The cellos played more aggressively. I loved it.

I suspected that I was listening to something that no-one had heard for many years and it felt special.

Sitting there in the cottage, listening to this lost recording, got me thinking about Drake and his ability to self-destruct. It acted as a wake-up call to me and I finished writing the piano track that evening.

I got in touch with Nick Drake's estate and played the recording to Cally, who looks after the estate. He confirmed that it was Drake, and a lovely recording at that, but also told me that handwriting on the box was probably not Drake's. It is a mystery to this day as to whose it might be and who had sent the tape in to Island.

It was arranged for Robert Kirby to come to the studio and listen to the recording. Although Robert was not responsible for the string arrangement on the version of Cello Song on Five Leaves Left, he was incredibly knowledgable about all of Drake's demo recordings. He was friendly and avuncular, and reminded me of Father Christmas. I enjoyed meeting him.

He settled down in the studio and I put the recording on. When the guitar came in, it was obvious from Robert's face that he did not recognise this particular version. Then, as Drake's voice came in, his eyes moistened. It felt very personal and I remember thinking that his face would have made a telling photograph.

Maybe I was watching a man who simply missed his friend. Robert had spent the previous few years talking about Drake and being interviewed about him, but here he was hearing something from a time when so much life should have been ahead of them. Sometimes it is easy to forget how young they both were when they collaborated on such terrific work.

'What a wonderful recording,' Robert said, and as he left he thanked me profusely for letting him hear it.

What a gentleman and what a nice guy. I would have liked to work with him and was delighted that, in the last few years of his life, Robert was finally recognised as being a special string arranger and began getting work with some terrific artists once again.

So what is this recording? Initially the estate told me that they didn't think it was a Joe Boyd/John Wood recording. So is it Nick and a friend working out how the arrangement should go during the writing process? Or is it, as had been suggested, one of the original demos sent to Joe Boyd with one of Nick's university friends playing? This now seems unlikely. There was also a suggestion that it is one of the lost John Peel BBC sessions, where Nick played Cello Song without a cellist, and that an arranger or cellist has sent it in to Island with their arrangement on top saying, 'this is what I do, sample my wares'. Again, we may never know.

I kept thinking about two significant figures in Drake's life. Joe Boyd, who had signed him, and John Wood, who encouraged Nick and became a friend, so I played the track to them to find out if either could shed light on it. Wood, the engineer, recognised it and remembered recording the guitar and vocals at Morgan Studios in North London some months before the Five Leaves Left sessions started at Sound Techniques Studio, but definitely does not recall recording a cellist or percussionist on it. Joe Boyd, Nick's producer, has no memory of ever being at Morgan Studios with Nick, but is pleased that they re-recorded the song later, preferring the simpler arrangement on the released version. The recording is over forty years old now so finding people who can remember a session from back then with accuracy becomes more and more difficult. Casting slightly further afield, Richard Hewson, who scored some of the first recorded arrangements for Nick's material told me that he didn't arrange it; and the other musicians on the released version didn't play on it. So the trail does start to run a bit cold. But, of course, maybe that doesn't matter. Maybe it's just a wonderful piece of abandoned music and its genesis is not important now.

Copyright laws means that it is not for me to broadcast or release the recording. Nick Drake's estate currently take the view that, as Nick isn't around to make decisions, they are reluctant to release anything that was possibly rejected back then by him. On top of that, there is a perfectly respectable version of Cello Song out there already. This may not please Nick Drake completists but, of course, it has to be respected. The estate have live recordings and variations of known songs that they have chosen not to release – and that is the way of it as things stand. It is nice to know that these things are out there though and that maybe one day we might get to hear at least some of them. The estate asked me to keep the tape safe so I put it aside as a curiosity, thinking little more about it until I heard about Robert Kirby's death in 2009.

Around about that time, I saw the documentary film Grizzly Man. Towards the end of the film, in an immensely disturbing scene, we see the director Werner Herzog listening on headphones to the sound of the real-life subject of the film, Timothy Treadwell, being killed by a grizzly bear. The audience is saved this misery, but maybe there is something even worse about watching somebody listening to something so obviously horrific than actually listening to it yourself.

This got me thinking: what would I *enjoy* watching people listening to? And in that moment the concept of *Strange Face* was born.

Despite not being a photographer, I decided I would go round Britain giving people the opportunity to be amongst the first 200 people to hear the lost recording in exchange for my photographing them listening.

My brother lent me a good camera. I had already transferred the tape on to a CD (thank goodness I had, as most of my tapes of that age are now unplayable) and put it into an old favourite CD Walkman, then grabbed a pair of headphones out of the studio along with a pen and some paper to jot down everything people said. I jammed it all into a rucksack and set off on my adventures.

The first dozen photographs I took were of people I knew, but as news of my discovery started to circulate and I began to receive email after email from fans asking to hear it or for copies that I couldn't provide, I knew the only responsible thing to do was to make it into an entirely random project. This is why my sister, one of Drake's biggest fans, has still not heard it to this day (sorry, Anne). At first I was apprehensive – it was a bizarre proposition, especially for an inexperienced photographer – but the second I stopped a lone cyclist and watched a smile appear on his face as he enthusiastically agreed to listen and to be photographed, I knew I wouldn't look back. It felt like a good thing to do.

I would visit people in their houses. I would stop them in the streets. I would accost them in fields or at the supermarket, whatever their age, whatever their profession, and ask them whether they would like to hear the recording. I would ask them irrespective of whether they knew Nick Drake's music or not, and I would record their thoughts and reactions at being amongst the first people in nearly forty years to hear Drake singing this unique, unreleased version of the song that starts with the two words, *Strange Face.*

This book contains some of the images and stories of the people I photographed. I would like to express my thanks to every one of them for being curious, and for being prepared to share their time and thoughts on many things, including the music of a man who, in my opinion, was one of the most extraordinarily gifted singer-songwriters of the twentieth century.

I have never done anything so stimulating, rewarding, fun and pleasurable in my entire working life.

About Nick Drake

Nicholas Rodney Drake (19 June 1948 – 25 November 1974) is hailed as one of the greatest singer-songwriters of the twentieth century. The Independent on Sunday has called him 'passionately adored', but this wasn't always the case. Nick Drake's transition from relative obscurity to cult hero is one of the most mysterious and intriguing stories of recent music history.

Drake spent the first years of his life on the Indian subcontinent before moving to the village of Tanworth-in-Arden in Warwickshire, England with his parents, Rodney and Molly, and his older sister, Gabrielle. He attended Eagle House School and Marlborough College before going up to Fitzwilliam College, Cambridge.

There was always music in the Drake household. At school Drake played piano, saxophone and clarinet, but by the age of 16 he had turned to the guitar. Like her son, Molly Drake wrote songs, and these appear to have influenced Drake's guitar tunings, writing and vocal phrasing.

Drake's recording career began in the late 1960s. His debut album Five Leaves Left came out in 1969. By 1972, he had recorded two more albums – Bryter Layter and Pink Moon. None of them sold well on initial release and his increasing reluctance to perform live or to give interviews didn't help sales.

In 1974, suffering from depression and insomnia, Drake died from an overdose at the age of 26. Whether this was accidental or not is disputed, but it is often said that his disappointment that his talent had not been recognised contributed to his death.

Drake's death went largely unremarked upon at the time, but gradually his work has been reassessed. He is now said to be among the most influential songwriters of the last 50 years, and the quintessentially English sound of Drake's spellbindingly accurate guitar playing, gentle voice and poetic lyrics excites great passion and loyalty.

It is said that when Drake's manager, Joe Boyd, sold his production company to Island Records he put a clause into the contract that ensured Drake's music would always be available. Patrick Humphries' and Trevor Dann's biographies kept the flame burning, and every year the number of Drake's fans grows. Over the years Rolling Stone magazine has put all three of his releases into their run-down of the 500 greatest albums of all time. A Radio 2 documentary narrated by Brad Pitt extended his appeal even further, and Drake's work now regularly features in films, television programmes and advertisements, bringing it to new audiences.

Photographs taken during his recording career show him to be a tall, handsome, elegant young man with shoulder length hair. The fact that, as of this moment, there is no known film footage of Drake apart from as a toddler adds to the artist's mystique.

In his short recording career Nick Drake had generated a legacy that would go on to influence some of pop's most high-profile artists and charm millions. Sadly, he did not live to enjoy his success.

"We are living in a world where recorded music is distributed so casually and freely it's almost lost its value. However, here was an opportunity to use a recording to create a very personal moment for a number of people and maybe give them an incredibly special memory."

Michael Burdett

'There is a beautiful sense of hope about that.'

```
Name: Rob, music shop assistant
Likes: various, especially John Martyn
Familiar with Nick Drake's music: Very
```

As I walked into a guitar shop on the outskirts of London and explained to Rob what I was doing he said two things.

1) 'Things like this don't actually happen.'
2) 'Hang on while I lock the door.'

He was not going to be disturbed as he seized the moment to listen and completely embraced his four minutes and twenty two seconds, sucking in every note, hum and twist and turn.

Afterwards he said, 'That was absolutely stunning. It was a quite simple but elegant arrangement.'

We talked a bit about music and Rob told me that he had been in various bands himself.

'Which band had the worst name?' I asked.

He didn't hesitate. 'There, There, Jane'.

I smiled, although secretly I quite liked it.

He unlocked the door, looking visibly moved by what had just happened. We shook hands and I walked out. Then I poked my head back round the door and told him that there was a queue outside consisting of many people with unreleased tracks by interesting artists ready for him to hear.

'Oh,' he said, 'send in the guy with the Jimi Hendrix tape first.'

'I prefer this version.'

```
Name: José, cinema manager
Likes: bosa nova, Astrud Gilberto,
       early Fleetwood Mac
Familiar with Nick Drake's music: Very
```

Having just watched the early evening screening of A Prophet, which had recently won the Grand Prix in Cannes and had been cited by some critics as the best French film for a decade, I asked the manager of the cinema, José, if he would like to hear the track.

What do you know, he was a big fan of Drake's work so he shut the door between the foyer and the cinema to ensure we would have privacy, asked one of his staff to keep the door closed, sat down and put the headphones on.

He recognised the differences in the recording, saying that he had thought it was a lovely version. Although we chatted about Drake for a few minutes afterwards, José seemed somehow distracted. Then I asked when the next showing of the film was on. 'Now,' he exclaimed, and with that he opened the door to the foyer only to find it absolutely rammed with people who had patiently been waiting for the doors to open.

Thank goodness they didn't know what had been keeping them, sardine-like, in the cinema entrance. I would only have made myself slightly more unpopular if I had told them that, in my opinion, they were not about to see the best French film for a decade.

'Do I have to listen to all of it?'

I stopped Louis during his lunch break when he was about to take his dog for a walk in Hyde Park, London. The quote beneath the picture is one of the first things he said after I put my offer to him. He was a man in a hurry.

This photograph was taken about one minute after he had put the headphones on. I stopped photographing but he carried on. In fact, he listened to it all.

'Wow, that was really good,' he said. 'It reminds me of Crosby, Stills and Nash.'

I took notes on everybody I stopped and I see that written on Louis' notes is the single word 'Floyd'. I can't remember if that is a reference to the fact that Louis likes the music of Pink Floyd or if Floyd is the dog's name. Anyway, we shook hands and off they both went, Louis and the dog that may or may not be called Floyd.

```
Name: Louis, art dealer
Likes: reggae, 70s rock
Familiar with Nick Drake's music: No
```

'It's psychedelic. It sounds almost Sergeant Pepperish.'

I don't think it is possible to know too much about music, but Laura comes close. During our conversation we talked of many styles. I mentioned the names of bands I imagined long forgotten, but she seemed fully aware of each Gypsy, Egg or Jericho Jones I referenced. She was familiar with all of Nick Drake's recordings too, which is great from someone born a while after his last album was recorded.

Leaning against a wall in West London, Laura looked down throughout the experience. She appeared absolutely transported while the track played and when she took the headphones off at the end she seemed genuinely startled.

'I loved it. I absolutely love it,' she said as she became aware of her surroundings again. 'I always think of him as being on his own but this sounds like a richer landscape. He sounds less isolated. It could have occurred at any time, like Keats.'

'It has elements of The Beatles' Within You Without You about it,' she said, just before going on to invent the word 'pepperish'.

Laura writes with genuine clarity, skill and passion about music and has described Nick Drake's music in print as being 'otherwordly'.

Judging by her look of astonishment as the track finished, I began to wonder if that's where people go when they are listening to him.

```
Name: Laura, writer, journalist
Likes: Bon Iver, Van Morrison
Familiar with Nick Drake's music: Very
```

'Some of Nick Drake's harmonies don't work, especially when there are flutes involved but here everything works.'

```
Name: Dez, storyteller
Likes: modern jazz, Gary Burton.
Familiar with Nick Drake's music: Yes
```

Dez runs a storytelling museum in Shropshire and when I turned up he insisted that he told me a story. No-one leaves his establishment without one, so I settled back and he wove dreams in my very head about princes and princesses, evil kings and subterfuge, love and deceit, revenge and peace. Then he put the headphones on.

'It sounds like he has been listening to Davy Graham,' he said afterwards. 'It has an Indian flavour to it and it makes me want to listen to him more. That is really, really good.'

I was introduced to Dez a couple of years earlier in the south of England at the funeral of a mutual friend and we worked out that although, we had never met before, the chap I used to buy my paper from when I lived in Wales was his son. This is not the biggest coincidence in the world but I figure it deserves a mention. So there is a story for you too. Nobody leaves this page without one.

'He sounds like he has deep issues. I have never heard anything like it.'

```
Name: Linda, care worker
Likes: Kirk Franklin, Jesus Culture, Marvin Sapp,
       Whitney Houston
Familiar with Nick Drake's music: No
```

Linda really enjoyed the recording and said that it was something you would have to listen to again because it causes you to think. She also thought that it was the sort of song where the words alone would be enough.

Linda works in a dementia unit at an old people's home and any break in her day that puts a smile on her face is entirely a good thing. I loved the fact that she got the giggles just towards the end of the track as it started to fade.

'It was like the forest came to life and carried me about in a little silver papoose.'

I guessed correctly that these two were fans of Nick Drake's work when I stumbled across them when I was on the way to a meeting. They crossed the road in front of me and I did a u-turn, got out of the car and said three things.

1) 'Do you like Nick Drake?'
2) 'Would you like to be among the first people to hear a 40-year-old-Nick-Drake recording in exchange for me photographing you doing so?'
3) 'Oh, by the way, I am not mental.'

When Noel started to listen to the track there was a moment when he touched his comedy partner's arm and said, 'It's that voice, that voice'.

'It sounds like a really good version. I actually preferred it to the original,' he said at the end. Then he suggested that I should get Brad Pitt to hear the recording because he is a really big Nick Drake fan.

I did, in fact, contact Brad Pitt's agent that night by phone. After listening to my offer, the woman who answered gave me an email address so I could send a written proposal. If you look through this book I think it will become obvious whether they came back to me or not.

```
Name: Noel, comedian, actor, musician and artist
Likes: The Rolling Stones, Syd Barrett,
       Captain Beefheart, Tangerine Dream
       and hip-hop
Familiar with Nick Drake's music: Very
```

'A lovely track. I really liked it. It had an Indian feel to it.'

I stopped a lady who was crossing the road in Ullapool in Scotland and asked if she would like to hear the recording. 'I really would, but I am late for school and as I am the teacher that wouldn't be a good thing, would it?' She did, however, direct me to a house where she said I would find Richard. 'He organises the guitar festival. I'm sure he would love to hear it, got to go, sorry.' And with that she disappeared.

I wandered towards the big white house and hoped I was going to find a guitar festival organiser and not some axe-wielding loon who had just been texted by his accomplice: 'Another victim on way, sharpen blade.'

The door was opened by Richard's wife, Colleen. She directed me into the back garden where I found Richard digging. Richard and Colleen were great company and we chatted for a good long time about the annual Ullapool Guitar Festival, which Richard organises. He proceeded to bring guitars for me to try, including a Fylde Magician acoustic, which was just astonishingly beautiful to play.

Eventually Richard and I moved back into the garden to remove ourselves from the noise of the washing machine. He put on the headphones and listened. 'Who did the orchestration?' he asked. 'It might possibly be Richard Hewson,' I tried, although I thought this was unlikely (confirmed at a later date when I met up with Hewson).

We continued chatting for a while and I felt so comfortable and welcome that I thought about asking if I could move in, but Richard had digging to do and a life to lead so I said goodbye and continued on my journey.

```
Name: Richard, guitar festival organiser
Likes: Little Feat, Average White Band, Ry Cooder,
       Robbie McIntosh, Andy Fairweather Low,
       Clive Carroll
Familiar with Nick Drake's music:  A bit
```

Sarah: *'Calming and beautiful.'*

Charlie: *'It's a very good song.
I didn't know it but I
could spot his unique voice.'*

Sarah removed her shoes then Charlie grabbed his elder sister's hand and off they went down the slope of the Turbine Hall at Tate Modern. This was possibly going to be a first, I thought: a Nick-Drake-inflicted accident. Charlie sped up and Sarah's stockinged feet allowed her to be towed at quite some speed as the track played. Thankfully, there was no crash. They zoomed past me at a heck of a pace and when they got to the bottom turned round, laughing, before walking back up the slope to do it again.

They stopped after the second descent and Sarah continued to listen. 'If I hadn't been being pulled down a slope and had heard the words, I am sure it would have been thought provoking too,' she said, 'but strangely, it was calming and beautiful.'

Charlie went next. He was aware of Drake's material but didn't know Cello Song, however, he recognised the voice immediately. 'It's incredible. It's a very good song,' he said. And off they went, this time walking and both in shoes.

```
Names: Sarah, student
       Charlie, student
Sarah likes:   Blink 182, Taking Back Sunday
Charlie likes: The Beatles, Led Zeppelin
Familiar with Nick Drake's music: A bit/A bit
```

'That was so different when the rhythm came in, I thought I could dance to this. It's so funky and loose.'

```
Name: Jason, care worker, Nick Drake fanzine
      editor
Likes: Paul Weller, The Beatles, The La's, Midlake,
       Nick Drake
Familiar with Nick Drake's music: Completely
```

If you are a fan of Nick Drake, then you should salute this man. From a very young age, Jason Creed helped keep the Drake flame alight by issuing the fanzine Pink (latterly Pynk) Moon between 1994 and 2000. The magazine came to an end when Jason realised that he had gone from knowing nothing to knowing everything about Nick Drake and had written about it all. 'I had gone full circle,' he said. In that time he interviewed and met many people who knew and had worked with Nick.

Jason introduced me to his young son, Alexander. Alexander will, I trust, grow up to be proud of his gentle, intelligent father who has done so much to inform and educate people about many aspects of Nick's life.

As I was leaving I asked Jason what it was that he liked most about Nick Drake.

'The guitar's the star,' he replied.

In 2012 the fanzine re-launched and is going strong once more.

'A minute after listening I had no idea what the lyrics were but it made me feel calm. It was trance-like. It makes me want to go and listen to Nick Drake more seriously.'

```
Name: Daniel, chess grandmaster
Likes: Miles Davis, Little Feat, Beatles, Bach,
       Latin, blues
Familiar with Nick Drake's music: A bit
```

I met Daniel at the London Chess Classic, which was the most prestigious chess tournament London had hosted for many years. It turns out that not only does Daniel play, write about, teach and commentate on chess but he is also an accomplished musician. He plays guitar, piano and double bass and is currently playing in 'a few different bands'.

He cited the three best gigs he had ever attended as The Stranglers at The Roundhouse in '77, Iggy Pop at The Lyceum in '80 and B.B King at The Hammersmith Odeon in '84. One day I will stop being so judgmental, but I have to admit that this was not what I was expecting from a chess grandmaster in a smart suit.

Daniel listened with his eyes tightly closed from beginning to end and, just to prove what a child I can be, seeing a chess grandmaster with his eyes shut in front of me and a pristine chess board set up between us, I moved the pieces so that it looked like I had him in check with my bishop.

Daniel was a little surprised at how much he enjoyed the track. 'It got into a groove very quickly and it never let up. It started off in an English folky way and then the next layer came in, which was Indian influenced and it never jarred. I thought it was fantastic. I loved it,' he said.

Daniel was excellent company and very knowledgeable about music. But I have to be honest, I was just as fascinated by his life as a grandmaster. 'I was marked out when I was young as having potential and it just went from there,' he explained. I asked if he ever took time off from chess. 'I once went two months without touching a piece,' he told me.

Maybe that is why I got him in check. Well, that and the fact he was learning to love Nick Drake and had no idea that we were playing.

'So cool.'

```
Name: Abby, dance teacher
Likes: modern British folk, Steve Reich,
       world music, Nick Drake
Familiar with Nick Drake's music: Yes
```

I walked into The Place, a contemporary dance school and venue in London, and walked up to the first floor, passing a number of students who were leaving one of the rehearsal rooms. Cheekily, I ventured inside and found Abby. When I told her what I was doing, a smile appeared on her face. It turns out that she was a real admirer of Nick Drake's material. 'I'm about to teach another group of students, when can I hear it?' she asked. 'How about now?' I replied.

A number of dancers for the next class were huddled outside the entrance to the studio so I went and told them that Abby was going to be busy for five minutes.

The room was quiet and filled with bright sunlight that flooded through the far windows. Initially, Abby just stood and listened, leaning against a desk, smiling as she held the CD player, but after about a minute she very quietly started to move. Slowly and gracefully, she walked around the room. It felt like the most natural thing in the world. Although I couldn't hear the music, her movements felt totally appropriate and I began to guess where in the song she might be from the way she was moving. There was nothing forced about her dancing, she just casually and elegantly meandered around, smiling.

'Beautiful,' she said eventually. 'That took me into a really calm meditative state. I was just enjoying moving around in the sun and being transported to another time.'

I opened the door and, like a tornado, eight energetic dancers noisily rushed in.

*'The great thing about
Nick Drake is that you
have to meet him halfway.
You've got to lean in
to hear what he's saying.'*

```
Name: Billy, musician
Likes: Jackson Browne, Tom Waits, Ry Cooder,
       Bob Dylan
Familiar with Nick Drake's music: Yes
```

How badly this encounter started. When Billy put on the headphones nothing happened. The fifteen-year-old CD player that had been through so much with me had packed up.

Billy had some filming to do in London so I set off to find an identical (for continuity purposes) CD player and we arranged to meet up later. I wasn't too hopeful.

I walked into the first electrical shop I came to in Tottenham Court Road (the Mecca of all things electronic in London) and there sitting in the display case was my exact same CD player. Not only that…it was in a box. Brand new but fifteen years old. I bought it and walked back to meet up with Billy.

He would probably be the first to admit that Nick Drake is possibly a bit too pastoral for his taste, but on a professional level he absolutely gets him. 'There is wonderful craftsmanship in his lyrics,' he said. 'There are elements of early Paul Simon there. Pre Bridge Over Troubled Water.'

'If I was living in a bed-sit aged 19 years old that song would have summed up my day.'

*'You must come to Moscow.
You are good.'*

Born in Uzbekistan and now living in Portugal, Westa is the daughter of artists and she got the project straightaway. I came across her as she was leaving an art gallery in London. She thought that the track was nice and calm and that it would make excellent travelling music.

Like a lot of people, she said that music is much more important to her than the lyrics. She liked the track a lot and insisted that I wrote Nick Drake's name on a piece of paper.

When she had finished listening to the track she asked if I would take a photograph of her on her own camera. This was the first time I realised that someone actually thought I might be a proper photographer rather than a bloke with a camera. It felt like a peculiar responsibility as I had to step up to the mark.

I looked through her viewfinder and clicked away. I got really lucky and the photograph looked excellent. That was the moment that Moscow seemingly opened its doors to me. Westa looked at the photograph and said, 'You must come to Moscow, you are good.'

Do I just turn up?

I am a photographer. It's official. Westa says so.

```
Name: Westa, tattoo artist and painter
Likes: The Prodigy, experimental, electro,
       drum and bass, country, blues
Familiar with Nick Drake's music: No
```

'Do you like that?'

```
Name: David, car park attendant
Likes: Madonna, Elton John, dance
Familiar with Nick Drake's music: No
```

'Would you like to put on some headphones and listen to a recording of a song that hasn't been heard for nearly forty years?' I asked David in the car park at Southampton airport. 'Yes please,' he said. 'I use an iPod a lot at home as it's nice to have something in your head.'

I asked what he meant and it turns out that David suffers from tinnitus. 'I wear in-ear headphones at home. It helps me escape,' he explained. Tinnitus is usually described as a ringing noise. In David's case it is buzzing and headphones offer relief, so for four minutes twenty two seconds Nick Drake was about to perform a really useful service.

'That is very calming,' David said at the end of the track. 'There are no electric instruments and you could relax to that.'

David then turned the question round on me: 'Do you like that?' he enquired.

'What I like most about this recording is the fact that it has given me the courage to approach complete strangers and that they have revealed themselves to be fascinating and almost universally kind,' I said.

'Oh, and the guitar.'

'He was 26 when he died?
Fucking hell. Poor man, or should I say poor boy?'

Evelyn – or Sparrow as she is more commonly known around the streets of west London – put on the headphones and listened to the track on a cold April Fool's Day morning. When she made the comment referring to Nick as a 'poor man, or should I say poor boy?' she had no idea that Nick Drake wrote a song called Poor Boy.

She sat silently on a seat outside a café while a number of refuse collectors noisily went about their work around us, but she wasn't to be distracted. Taking off the headphones, she remarked that it was nice just to have slightly warmer ears for a few minutes.

'He sounded much older,' she said when I told her Nick's story. 'And the lyrics were really good. It's very folky. If I was in the money, I would buy that.'

As an aside, a couple of years ago I had a tax bill that had me reeling. After paying it, I bumped into Sparrow. I must have looked especially glum because she asked me what the matter was. When I told her, she delved into her pocket and pulled out the most crumpled five pound note I had ever seen. Pointing at Starbucks she said, 'Go inside, relax and get yourself a coffee.'

If the least I did on the day she heard the track was warm up her ears for a few minutes, it was something. Sparrow has a good heart and she always makes me smile.

```
Name: Evelyn, not currently working
Likes: Gypsy Kings, Beethoven, Mozart,
       popular music
Familiar with Nick Drake's music: No
```

'This music is not so good for the street when you are performing, but when you are relaxing it is good.'

Name: Rudi, street performer
Likes: Mozart, 'Queen are best'
Familiar with Nick Drake's music: No

Rudi paints himself gold and dresses up in Tudor costume to perform on the streets of London. I came across him on the South Bank, near the Millennium Wheel. It was quite hard for him to hear the music because our surroundings were noisy, but he posed and sashayed around to the track, bowing and being generally splendid. Go see him and be generous. He does an extraordinary thing very beautifully

'Très bonne.'

**Name: Sall, fishery worker
Likes: Spanish, African and French music
Familiar with Nick Drake's music: No**

I was in Lochinver, a fishing port in Assynt in Scotland. Walking along the road towards me was Sall and I asked if he would like to listen to a recording of Nick Drake. As Sall explained as best he could that he couldn't understand me, it became apparent that he was from Spain and spoke little English. I, in turn, speak no Spanish. It looked as though we were stuck. But then I had a brainwave. 'Parlez vous Francais?' I tried. 'Oui, un peut,' he replied. This was good, I thought, now I could explain what I was doing and see if Sall fancied putting the headphones on.

There was a problem, however. I suddenly realised that pretty much all my schoolboy French had left me. However hard I tried, I could not explain the finer points of what I was doing. Sall explained in a combination of Spanish, French and English that he was a fishery worker and that he was working on board one of the large Spanish fishing boats that was in the harbour but that was about as far as we got. Stalemate again.

Then I had another brainwave. There is a telephone text service that claims to answer any question you have. So I texted the number 63336 and asked them to translate my Nick Drake photographic question into French. Thankfully, there was plenty of signal so the answer came back within a couple of minutes. I showed the phone to Sall and he read the following…
Je voyage a travers le pays, prendre des photographies de personnes qui sont a l'ecoute d'une recemment decouvert chanson. Puis-je vous photographier?

He nodded in agreement but still had a couple of questions. Luckily, I remembered Christelle, a French friend of mine, was in the area so I phoned her and she explained the finer details of the project to Sall.

Now, there are a number of flaws with my approach. I am sure you have spotted them. I felt more stupid than a stupid man from the Planet Stupid when I realised later what I had done. Why didn't I ask 63336 to send the text in Spanish or phone a Spanish friend so that poor Sall wasn't permanently having to translate?

I was genuinely ashamed that a grammar school educated boy (me) was such an idiot. But Sall was patient and smiled his way through all my idiocy and spoke much better French than I did. In fact, his English (his third – or possibly fourth – language, as he had explained that he was from Africa originally) was better than my French. He put on the headphones and listened while leaning against the railings with the sea behind him. This moment seemed to cement our strange relationship and it became most enjoyable watching him as he kept turning back and smiling at me throughout.

He spoke at the end and smiled as though he had enjoyed the track, but I couldn't really understand what he was saying, except for little smatterings of French. And, of course, it didn't matter. We had muddled along in our own fashion, communicating quite nicely in a number of different ways. We shook hands and, as a parting shot, he pointed at the headphones then put the first two fingers of his right hand together with his thumb, touched them to his lips and kissed them away in that age old sign of approbation. Does that hand gesture have a name? I decided there and then to always refer to it as a Salloot. Oh, and to learn another language – properly.

'The song lacks a climax.'

```
Name: Julia, cellist
Likes: classical, jazz
Familiar with Nick Drake's music: No
```

It was obvious that I had to stop Julia because she was walking along with a cello. Also, I always feel sorry for cellists because, along with double basses, bassoons and pole-vault poles, cellos are as awkward to carry as anything, so it seemed like a good thing to give her a break.

Julia is from Holland and is studying music in the UK. She had not heard of Nick Drake and she didn't seem overly impressed. The track was sometimes a bit too mellow, she told me, and it could have ended better. When I asked about her musical tastes she seemed reluctant to mention any specific classical composers, saying 'there are too many.'

She may not have cared for the track much but she was incredibly game, battling away in the wind, listening while trying to support her cello and keeping the headphones in place.

'Very pleasant, melodious. Jolly good.'

```
Name: John, retired
Likes: Henry Hall, Victor Silvester
       and 'good quality light music'
Familiar with Nick Drake's music: No
```

At the age of 96 John was the most senior person I photographed. His hearing is not as good as it was, so he tends not to listen to as much music as he once did.

I have known John since I was very young and have loved listening to his opinions on all sorts of music over the years. John's son has produced some of the heftiest of heavy metal bands, worked with operatic singers, and has mixed tracks with vocals by singers ranging from Lou Reed to Emmylou Harris. This means that, by proxy, music of all sorts has been a part of John's life. 'In the early days I built amplifiers,' he said just before he put on the headphones.

After a false start when he had to adjust his hearing aid, the track started. John kept time with the palm of his hand on the arm of his chair whenever the cellos played. 'Very good, Micky,' he said as it came to an end (he is one of only two people who call me this). 'That was thoroughly pleasant.' As is John.

'I could listen to that in the car.'

```
Name: Keith, entrepreneur
Likes: house, dance
Familiar with Nick Drake's music: No
```

Keith was walking along with a couple of other guys dressed like this and my guess was that they were extras at the nearby A stage at Pinewood studios during the filming of the remake of Swift's Gulliver's Travels, starring Jack Black. As I chatted to Keith, I asked what he did for a living. 'Entrepreneur,' he responded.

'That is nice and chilled. I could listen to that in the car,' Keith told me after removing the headphones. He shook my hand then he and his colleagues went off in search of an entirely different vehicle: the catering van. As they started to walk away, Keith stopped and turned round with a big smile on his face. 'Is there any money in this for me?' he asked.

Now that is true entrepreneurial spirit.

'The track was very good.'

Name: Rob, farmer
Likes: 'any old shit'
Familiar with Nick Drake's music: No

Rob is a hard-working farmer and a lovely bloke. In his own words, he is 'generally too pre-occupied with other things, so I don't really do music. I don't really identify with it.'

I managed to convince him to put on the headphones, though. Even so, he continued to work, unable to stay still. At one point he started to climb into a huge digger and I worried that the second he fired the engine up the mellow sounds of Nick Drake in his ears would disappear under the noise. Eventually Rob handed back the headphones. 'The track was very good,' he said. And then he added, 'peaceful'. It made me laugh. The whole episode had looked anything but.

'It had a similar folksy, beatnik vibe
to something I saw Kirsty Wark
tapping her feet to on
Newsnight Review recently.'

```
Name: David, advertising agency owner
Likes: Ray Charles, B.B. King
Familiar with Nick Drake's music: No
```

'I don't listen to enough music really,' David replied when I asked him what sort he liked. 'Today I've mostly been listening to this.' He pointed to his computer and a screen showing Tony Blair being quizzed at the Iraq War Inquiry.

I offered him the headphones.

While he listened he continued to work, reading a document that he was proofing. 'Nice track,' he said when it came to an end. 'I don't really know much about Nick Drake.'

I gave him a potted history but his eyes kept going back to the computer. 'Blair has a great defence,' he said. 'Which is essentially *I thought I was right*. I'm sure both Pol Pot and Hitler would have used that one.'

I left that little bit of the real world and went to find my next headphone wearer.

'I used to think his music was melancholy but now I know his music is sweet, innocent and pure.'

```
Name: Peta, multi-dimensional spokeswoman for the
      spiritual hierarchy
Likes: all kinds of music from opera to jazz to
       ska to thrash metal - and Michael Franti
       & Spearhead
Familiar with Nick Drake's music: Very
```

As I drove towards the south coast, I thought it might be nice to get a photograph or two with the sea in the background. The sun was shining and the sky seemed exceptionally blue. But when the sea came into view, with it came the most incredibly dense sea mist which all but obliterated the water from sight. I stopped at some traffic lights and engaged in conversation with a pedestrian, telling him I was going to the seaside to photograph people in headphones. 'Is that normal?' I asked, indicating to the mist. 'No,' he replied, adding, 'and I've lived here for about twenty years.' He then leaned towards his companion, saying, 'I've never seen anything as thick as that.' I hoped he was talking about the mist, although he seemed to be pointing at me.

I liked Peta's thoughts on the track very much but was scared to ask for the meaning of the quote that accompanies this photograph. Given her spiritual hierarchy connections, she would probably have told me that she had popped over to the other side and asked Nick, 'So are you melancholy then, or what?' And this, quite frankly, would scare me just a tad too much.

'I like the way he starts off in E minor and switches straight to B, which is a nice way of starting the tune. I like the blend of strings and guitar that doesn't need bass and drums to sustain it. There is something about that voice that strikes a chord. He sings very softly but there is an undercurrent of deep feeling. It is very soothing but at the same time thought-provoking. It's a shame the conductor of my orchestra is not here to listen as he would give you a much better informed opinion than I can.'

```
Name: Mark, nuclear safety case engineer
Likes: Scottish folk music, heavy rock,
       Cappercaillie, Thunder, Deep Purple, Toto,
       Wolfstone
Familiar with Nick Drake's music: No
```

I went up this mountain, Stac Pollaidh in the Scottish Highlands, with Mark but he had no idea that I was intending to ask him if he wanted to hear the track when we got to the top. We walk up a mountain every year. Well, I wheeze my way up and he marches. He comes from a family of mountaineers, plays the viola in an amateur orchestra, and it would appear has perfect pitch. Mark's modest statement that his orchestra leader would have come up with a better critique under these mountain top circumstances is, I suspect – and I mean no disrespect to the conductor – unlikely.

'*Come on, come on and dance with me.*'

```
Name: Giovanni, fashion consultant
Likes: soul, rock and roll
Familiar with Nick Drake's music: No
```

Giovanni embraced his moment in a different way from everyone else. Once he had found the groove, he approached a group of people at a bus stop and started twirling, clapping his hands and gyrating gently. He was trapped in a musical world dancing to Nick Drake, which is a sentence I never thought I would get to write in my life.

Giovanni's attitude was infectious so for a moment I danced with him in order that he had at least one partner. I suspect that Giovanni may well be one of the world's natural dancers. I am not. A bus pulled up and a new group of potential dance partners tumbled off it. Giovanni smiled, twisting and clapping louder. 'Come on… dance,' he cried.

'I could stand here listening to that all day.'

```
Name: Lynne, advocate for women's empowerment
Likes: troubador music, world music, Neil Young,
       Joni Mitchell, Nick Drake, Bob Dylan,
       Leonard Cohen, African music, Indian music,
       Brazilian music.
Familiar with Nick Drake's music: Yes
```

Walking along behind Lynne was Harry, her assistant, who was piled high with bags of food, his arms full to breaking point. Also threaded on his arm was a lead and the dog at the end of it was nearly tripping him up. Lynne seemed to be carrying little.

I liked the look of women's empowerment and I thought about kicking Harry, just to show her whose side I was on

Lynne turned out to be really delightful company, and hilarious, but when I explained what I was doing, she got the wrong end of the stick, thinking I was trying to sell her a Nick Drake bootleg CD or something of the sort. All was put right when I showed her a couple of photographs. She put the headphones on while Harry went off on an errand.

As Lynne leaned against a wall heavy with graffiti, she looked for all the world as though she was in heaven. Around her Notting Hill was getting ready for the carnival, but she stayed still, ignoring the activity. 'One of the greatest 20th century poets and songwriters,' she proclaimed as she took off the headphones. 'Time for another revival.'

'I immediately went somewhere else,' she continued. 'I could stand here listening to that all day. What a waste. What a shame he is no longer here.'

Harry re-appeared and off they went. I noticed that Lynne was now carrying some of the bags. One Nick Drake track and she has forgotten the art of empowerment, I thought. Harry nodded and smiled at me. What a fun few minutes.

'I was quite impressed.
It was very soothing.
I could listen to that.
There was nothing harsh about it.'

Name: Pete, college porter
Likes: Beatles, Pink Floyd, Queen
Familiar with Nick Drake's music: No

Pete was everything a college porter should be: friendly with an air of discipline and strength about him. As he took up 'the easy position', I wondered if he had a military background. He was one of a number of people to suggest that Nick Drake would be very easy to listen to with a glass of wine by your side while sitting in a comfy chair. 'I could definitely listen to a whole album like that,' he said.

*'Very pleasing.
His music demands that you listen.
It is quite complex.'*

Name: Ashley, company director
Likes: Snow Patrol to Woody Guthrie.
       'In fact all Guthries are good.'
Familiar with Nick Drake's music: Yes

I caught Ashley in the changing rooms of my squash club. Until then I had no idea how angry naked men can get when you start using flash photography in a changing room. However, as they disappeared into the showers, Ashley put the headphones on.

He did not know Cello Song and told me it sounded 'spiritual', adding 'with his combination of lyrics and melody you have no option but to listen.'

Men started re-appearing so I put the camera and CD player away and, grabbing a towel, walked into the showers with Ashley. As we soaped ourselves, we chatted more about music. Then I remembered I hadn't even played yet.

'Wow. It's enabled me to rediscover a song I already knew and wonder about the process of how this version came about.'

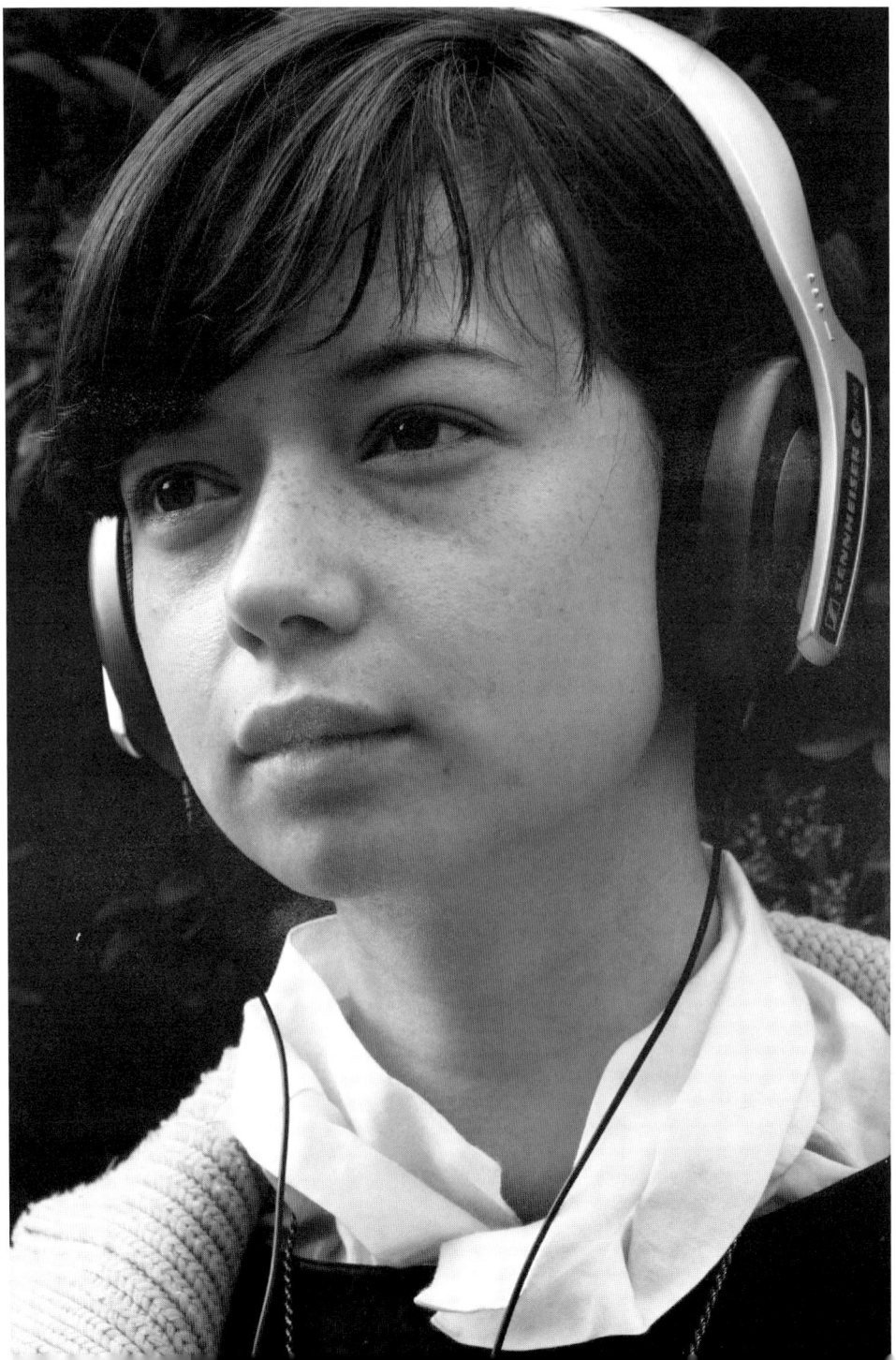

```
Name: Lucinda, photographer/musician
Likes: Bach, Ravel, Satie, Bonnie Prince Billy,
       Cat Power
Familiar with Nick Drake's music: Yes
```

Lucinda, a photographer, musician and Nick Drake fan, was intrigued about the recording. 'It sounded familiar to start with,' she said, 'but when the strings came in with a shimmering tremelando it felt different, which was interesting as it set it apart from Cello Song as I know it.' Lucinda said she had never really connected with 'proper British Folk music' but loves Nick Drake because 'he is so accessible'.

We talked a good deal about when the recording might have been done and under what circumstances.

'It's enabled me to rediscover a song I already knew and wonder about the process of how this version came about,' she said.

She was also really helpful on the subject of photography and seemed to like what I was doing.

I have since checked out some of Lucinda's photography and she would appear to be rather good. Gulp.

'If you'd had a shitty day you could get a glass of wine or a beer, sit in a comfy chair, put your feet up, lay back, relax and listen to that. It's smashing.'

Steve – or Browny as he is more commonly known – runs a fishing tackle shop which always reminds me of Desmond's from the Channel Four comedy series. Like the Peckham hairdresser's, there are always numerous visitors sitting around on chairs, drinking coffee and chatting. I didn't think donning the headphones would be Steve's kind of thing, so when he showed keen interest I was surprised.

The second he started to listen Steve seemed to turn into a man I barely recognised. He became still and looked reflective and, dare I say it, moved. This was not the tough old tackle vendor I knew at all but a sensitive, sweet-looking, vulnerable guy.

When the track finished, I gave him a potted history of Nick's life story. 'It sounds to me like the world has lost a real star. If he'd been around longer he would have gone all the way,' said Steve. 'I lost my son, you know. He was the light of my life.'

Now it was me who was hearing something new. We shook hands as I left. In barely five minutes all that I felt and thought I knew about Steve had flipped on its head.

Name: Steve, fishing tackle dealer
Likes: Tamla Motown, The Stylistics
Familiar with Nick Drake's music: No

'That was my moment of relaxation for the day.'

```
Name: Ireneo, fashion student
Likes: PJ Harvey, Fleetwood Mac, Patti Smith,
       Stevie Nicks
Familiar with Nick Drake's music: Yes
```

As I stopped Ireneo I realised that he was a man in a hurry who was possibly not having the best of days. He was walking along with a friend and I am guessing that I created tension between them when I gave Ireneo (a big Nick Drake fan) the opportunity to listen to the track. Ireneo's companion went off with what could have been construed as a terse 'I'll see you later, then.'

The next five minutes seemed to transform Ireneo. I watched as he moved from tense to still to relaxed. Although we were just yards from one of London's busiest thoroughfares, the sidestreet we were standing in seemed to miraculously empty. 'That was lovely,' he said afterwards. 'Thank you.'

We shook hands and he and his magnificent oversized safety pin disappeared into the busy London streets.

'When you listen to music on headphones and it becomes a soundtrack to what is happening around you, it is like watching a live-action video. I really liked it.'

Ross lost most of his personal possessions in the Australian bushfires of 2009 and has now moved back to the UK with his wife and young daughter. I saw him walking through Soho in London and was taken by how dashing his motor cycle leathers made him look. I approached and asked if he knew of Nick Drake and if he would like to hear the recording. He said yes, but all the time that he was leaning against his bike listening a traffic warden was hovering around. Ross seemed nervy about the warden and it turned out that he did not have a valid parking ticket. Naughty, naughty Ross, but – to be honest – if you have lost your personal possessions in a bush fire I think you should be excused parking tickets for the rest of time.

Incidentally, while he listened I spoke to the warden and asked him to ignore the ticketless bike and he readily agreed. This is not the expected behaviour of traffic wardens, so good on him.

Ross declared the whole listening experience very 'filmic'. He added that he really liked the recording but found what I was doing to be 'really odd'. I thought this was rich coming from a man who once rounded off his comedy set at a festival by leading a huge conga line (which quickly turned into a stampede) to a vegan food stand so they could all ask for pies and sausage rolls.

```
Name: Ross, comedian
Likes: The Beatlesons, accordion rock,
       Half Man Half Biscuit, Eels, The White Stripes
Familiar with Nick Drake's music: Yes
```

'It was just lovely, thank you, thank you.'

I stopped Samad as he was walking along a north London street. Within moments of putting the headphones on, he looked like a man transported and seemed quite moved by the experience.

Samad was one of the earlier participants to hear the recording and photographing him drove home to me the peculiar nature of what I was doing. Here was a man being stopped in the street by a stranger and asked if he would like to listen on headphones to a song by a man he had never heard of while the stranger took photographs. It was hardly an everyday experience. Yet it seemed to be the most natural thing in the world for both of us. I felt comfortable because I suspected that Samad was enjoying this strange little moment in his day. And the reason that I suspected that Samad felt good about the whole experience was because every time Nick Drake started humming so did he. Beautifully, gently and in tune.

```
Name: Samad, retired
Likes: Persian and Turkish music 'is most relaxing'
Familiar with Nick Drake's music: No
```

'It is perfect for this landscape – a bleak, desolate setting, but in a kind of romantic way.'

```
Name: Diane, ecommerce manager
Likes: Elbow, Belle and Sebastian, Coldplay, Keane,
    Madonna
Familiar with Nick Drake's music: No
```

Parked up in a field on the sea front in their campervan near the village of Achiltibuie in Northern Scotland were Diane and Craig. They were having a few days away touring round the Highlands. Although not familiar with Nick Drake, they embraced the idea of hearing some new music straightaway.

Diane leaned against a bench with her back to the sea, looked up at the hills, and put the headphones on. She listened in silence and a gentle smile appeared on her face. 'It's not what I was expecting,' she told me at the end. 'It sounds contemporary. I could imagine that being released today and doing really well.'

A few months later I got in touch with Diane by email as I had neglected to make a note of her musical tastes and I asked if she remembered our encounter.

She wrote back saying that although she is always a little self conscious about being photographed, she found it an interesting and pleasant interlude, both to find out about Nick and to listen to the track. She particularly remembered the music befitting the scenery and when she is next back on that beach she will be sure to listen to Cello Song again.

Diane now owns several Drake recordings. This filled me with delight.

'Really excellent. Quite emotional really.'

```
Name: Daniel, interactive arts student
Likes: The Tallest Man On Earth
Familiar with Nick Drake's music: No
```

I met Daniel outside the Museum of Everything, which at the time was showing stunning work by artists and creators living outside mainstream society. In his rockabilly clothing, Daniel was incredibly smart and I just wanted to applaud his hair. It was as crisp and as sharp as anything.

Like a number of people I photographed, his hand went to his mouth as he listened. I am no body-language expert but I found it an interesting phenomenon. Daniel said that Nick Drake's music reminded him of The Tallest Man On Earth, a Swedish folk singer he likes.

He told me that he found listening to the track 'a little bit moving' and I told him I wanted his hair.

It didn't sound as creepy when I said it to him as it does now that it is written down.

*'It made me drift away,
like sinking into my lover's arms.'*

```
Name: Peta, folk singer, librarian
Likes: jazz, folk
Familiar with Nick Drake's music: A bit
```

Cecil Sharpe House is the home of British folk music and Peta Webb is not only a traditional English folk singer but the resident librarian there. As the music started, her hand went to her knee and her foot looked like it desperately wanted to stomp on the wooden floor in time with the music. The track didn't let it happen, though.

'It's not folk music at all. It's acoustic music. It has little to do with traditional folk,' she said when it came to an end. 'It is certainly more akin to the sort of music that The Incredible String Band used to do.'

I had the impression that she was not keen, but as I had approached her in the home of folk she seemed to be viewing it from a folk perspective. Then she described how listening to the track with her eyes closed had taken her away to a romantic place. 'That is why I listen to jazz,' she continued 'It's about escape and romance, taking you to a more challenging place.'

I have just watched Peta on the internet performing from nearly thirty years ago. She would appear to be as folk as folk can be and as well as being the real deal is absolutely excellent to boot.

*'It calmed me down and relaxed me.
It reminded me of African tribal music – and Sade.'*

```
Name: Ken, chartered accountant
      ('but hedge fund manager if this book takes a
      while to come out')
Likes: hip hop, r&b, Jay Z
Familiar with Nick Drake's music: No
```

Ken is one of a number of people who said that the track reminded them of the music from their place of birth. He was talking about Africa but people from Ireland, Iraq, Scotland, Turkey, Wales, Malaysia, England, Iceland, Canada and India also told me they were reminded of the music of their roots. I loved the fact that Ken asked me when the project would see the light of day as this would alter his job title. He is a man who looks forwards. I, on the other hand, am also moving forward but, like a rower, I seem to be permanently looking backwards.

'I watched the sun move to this. It relaxed me.'

Just up from British Camp on The Malvern Hills I encountered Helen and her husband, Andy. I asked Helen what she did and was delighted to welcome my first cytotechnologist into the headphones.

Just in case you were wondering, cytotechnology is the study and interpretation of human cells to detect abnormalities. It could include samples from many areas of the body, including the uterine cervix, lung, gastrointestinal tract or body cavities, I seem to remember.

Anyway, Helen took a seat on the grass at the top of a winding path and started to listen. 'Melancholy,' she said afterwards (only the second time the M word had cropped up). 'It sounds like Jeff Buckley.' At the end of a delightful half an hour in the company of Helen and the playful Andy, she uttered my favourite of her statements: 'It sounds like meandering music.' However, I meandered off wondering why Helen stopped liking AC/DC.

```
Name: Helen, cytotechnologist
Likes: Robbie Williams, Michael Bublé,
     'I used to like AC/DC'
Familiar with Nick Drake's music: No
```

'I like a little puff in the afternoon and that would complement it perfectly. I could listen to him all day.'

```
Name: Steve, curtain installer
Likes: soul, Tamla Motown, disco, reggae
Familiar with Nick Drake's music: No
```

During the summer decorated elephants were placed all around the streets of London to bring attention to the plight of the Asian elephant. Eventually most of the 258 were brought to the Royal Hospital Chelsea to be auctioned off and that is where I found Steve staring at the brightly coloured pachyderms.

He wasn't aware of Nick Drake but really enjoyed the track. I got the feeling the experience would inspire him to find out more, although he may just have gone home, taken to a comfy armchair, lit up a big one, and thought it was all – elephants, Nick Drake, headphones – a dream.

'Happy, happy music. In fact, all music is happy anyway.'

```
Name: Bridie, retired caterer
Likes: Elton John, Smooth Radio
Familiar with Nick Drake's music: No
```

Bridie was magnificent. We sat on a bench and chatted for quite a while before I explained what I was doing and she asked if she could hear the track. She was pleased to be photographed as she had just had her hair done.

I was interested in her belief that all music was happy and thought about lending her City of Needles by The Legendary Pink Dots, but with her infectious enthusiasm and optimism she would have probably found joy in that too.

'Nick Drake, like Jeremy Clarkson, is unique and hence beyond criticism.'

Although not a particular fan of Nick Drake, Paul has a sister who is, so he was aware of his music. Despite not being that keen on having his photograph taken generally, he obligingly sat on a bench in a park near his London home, put on the headphones and listened to the track. He admitted to being slightly distracted by a cat ('in a good way') during what he called an 'unusual but positive experience'.

'He sounds quite a lot like Colin Blunstone,' he said afterwards before continuing, 'Nick Drake is almost like a cliché. A fey, uber-sensitive, not very interesting sixth former, who turns out to be the real deal.'

When I left Paul I told him I was off to go fishing and I was reminded of something he once said about his, and my, favourite pastime.

'Fishing consists of long periods of boredom occasionally interrupted by short, sharp periods of boredom.'

I left him with a smile on my face, confident that I had just heard the names Nick Drake and Jeremy Clarkson appearing together in a sentence for the very first time. What was especially serendipitous was that within a few weeks I came across Jeremy Clarkson in the street where I live. Of course, Paul's comment about Clarkson ringing in my ears made me duty bound to approach him.

```
Name: Paul, comedian, actor and writer
Likes: Paul Weller, The Sex Pistols,
       Mumford and Sons
Familiar with Nick Drake's music: Yes
```

'I felt like I was welling up, to be honest.'

```
Name: Bethany, musician
Likes: folk, Judee Sill.
Familiar with Nick Drake's music: Yes
```

I had just watched Bethany play the cello at a folk festival when I approached her. Did she know Nick Drake's material? Of course she did. She likes English folk but much prefers playing it to listening to it and has performed with many artists including Peter Gabriel, Eliza Carthy and the guitarist Newton Faulkner.

She sat under a tree, away from the main stage, and put on the headphones. I continually found it amazing that I could approach a stranger and in a matter of minutes be recording a really private emotional moment between them and an artist who had died over thirty five years previously. What, I wondered, would Nick Drake have thought if someone had told him that one day things like this would happen and that tribute concerts celebrating his work would be staged, with his songs being performed by many world-class acts.

'Wow, that's amazing,' said Bethany as she took the headphones off. 'It's really warm and there's a depth to it.' We chatted some more and she talked of her relationship with Cello Song. 'It's different listening to it on headphones. It really takes you to a different place. I felt like I was welling up, to be honest.' With that she went and got her mother, who she had insisted needed to listen.

'This makes me think of bows and bonnets and girls in Laura Ashley dresses.'

I have known David for some decades. When I first met him he was revelling in his love of punk and The Sex Pistols. He still is a big fan of punk and really likes the recordings of Paul Weller and The Jam, but points out that although The Jam were often bracketed together with the likes of The Sex Pistols, The Damned and The Clash they were not really part of the punk scene.

David knew much more about Nick Drake's life story than his music. 'This was very nice and free flowing. It made me feel easy and relaxed,' he said.

He remained absolutely still throughout the four minutes and twenty two seconds. This is the longest time I have ever known David to be quiet. He can be very loud and delightfully over-enthusiastic. I am also used to seeing David casually dressed. In his tie and in that kitchen setting, however, he reminded me more of Gilbert… or George than David.

```
Name: David, court usher
Likes: The Smiths, and 'everything from
       The Stone Roses to Clifford T Ward'
Familiar with Nick Drake's music: A bit
```

'You have made my day, that was just wonderful.'

```
Name: Geoff, retired jewellery seller
Likes: blues, Tamla Motown, soul
Familiar with Nick Drake's music: Yes
```

I came across Geoff in a mid Wales high street. He was very keen to listen as he really likes Nick Drake's work. He was standing in an alleyway which was called Bear Passage. It had a sign above it saying so. I am sure that even Geoff would recognise that there is an element of Grizzly Adams about his looks. I was trying hard to find an angle that would show Geoff and the sign above but then I looked through the lens and I thought: why bother? He just looked content and deep in contemplation, so I clicked away.

Sometimes people would hum as the track played. Geoff was one of those, humming quietly and endearingly in tune.

'I don't think I will be going to buy any Nick Drake.'

I was fishing on a remote Scottish beach that had taken quite a bit of map reading and walking to locate. It was a good mile or so from the nearest road and that road was barely a track. I caught a dab, a flatfish, which I decided to eat later.

I was not expecting to see anyone else that day but as I was about to pack up a kayak came into sight and two people made their way up on to the beach. We got chatting and it turned out they were working their way round a section of the coastline. Despite not being familiar with Nick Drake, Alison showed interest in hearing the track.

'His voice was a bit sentimental and croony and the percussion was a bit busy but it was quite a pleasant experience,' she told me at the end. 'It felt like feel-good music but I don't think I will be going to go and buy any Nick Drake.'

However, it was the next thing she said that particularly resonated with me. 'I found myself wanting to sing along. There was one line in the lyric…' and then she hesitated, looked around, and after a while said '…that I can't remember'.

I asked if she could remember any of the lyrics. She couldn't. We said goodbye and I spent my time walking back to the car trying to remember the lyrics to Cello Song, a song I had heard hundreds of times. And I couldn't. Not a thing beyond the first line. What on earth is that about? I needed brain food. Fish is brain food I remembered. Damn, I had just given my dab to a kayaker with a primus stove.

```
Name: Alison, social work lecturer
Likes: early music, Tallis, baroque, world, folk
Familiar with Nick Drake's music: No
```

Steven – *'He has now got the fame he always wanted but was too shy to achieve.'*

Nikki – *'I feel very lucky.'*

```
Name: Steven, company director
Name: Nikki, marine scientist
Steven likes: Queens of The Stone Age, Radiohead,
    Soul Saviours
Nikki likes: Björk, Massive Attack
Familiar with Nick Drake's music: Very/Very
```

Steven and Nikki were walking towards me arm in arm by a lock on the River Thames in Surrey as the sun faded away one wintry evening.

In the gloom I seemed to have found two Nick Drake aficionados. They were really knowledgeable about his work and both were really keen to hear the recording.

Nikki looked up at the birds gathering in the darkening sky while she listened and when it came to Steven's turn to be photographed she pressed her ear against one of the headphones. A moment after this shot was taken, with Steven still listening, they pulled apart, looked into each others eyes and kissed gently. And if you needed any proof that I am not a proper photographer, I became a tad embarrassed and turned the camera off.

'Beautiful. Whoever recorded it knew what they were doing.'

```
Name: Chris, buys, restores and sells vintage
            guitars
Likes: Mike Hedges, John Fahey
Familiar with Nick Drake's music: Very
```

This project would probably never have happened had it not been for Chris, although he wouldn't know that. Chris was the first person I photographed who I didn't know. I stopped him because I liked his bike. I leaned out of my car window and asked if he knew the music of Nick Drake. He said that he did and I told him that I had an unreleased version of Cello Song and that my intention was to photograph 200 people listening to it. Much to my amazement, Chris pulled an iPod out of his pocket and went to the Nick Drake section. It soon became obvious that he had every one of Drake's tracks that had ever been released, including all the out-takes and home recordings. Satisfied that he only had the one version of Cello Song from Five Leaves Left on the player he said, 'You'd better park your car, then.'

Talking to Chris and the way he embraced the whole process made me realise how easy it was going to be to get people to agree to my strange proposition. The project changed from a mad idea into something I might enjoy.

The fact that he turned out to be a man who restores and sells vintage guitars seemed especially serendipitous.

'Listening to Nick Drake always makes me nostalgic for things that didn't actually happen to me, like standing in a wheat field in Cambridge, which I've never done.'

```
Name: Robin, comedian and writer
Likes: Billy Bragg, Wild Beasts, Nick Cave
Familiar with Nick Drake's music: Very
```

Of all the quotes that people came out with this one certainly resonated with me. I liked giving Robin the opportunity to listen as I had recently heard him on radio describing how he had lost his extensive vinyl collection in a deluge of leaking sewage from his neighbour's property.

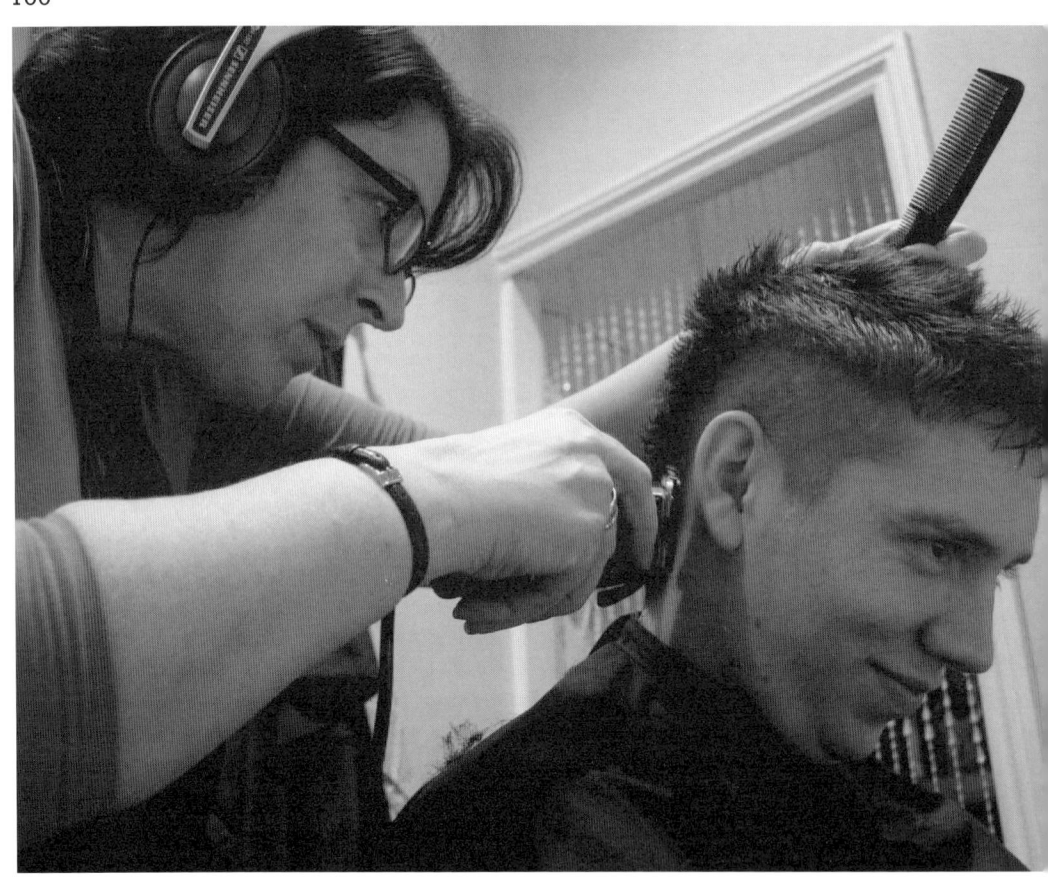

'We get requests to do strange things in this shop. It helps to break the day up.'

A Mohican haircut must be a relatively unusual haircut for someone to sport in the suburbs of Middlesex. I hope that that is what Jack had gone in for and Ada's concentration hadn't slipped for a moment as she became lost in the music.

After she removed the headphones, she was full of praise for the recording and amazed that she had never heard the name Nick Drake before.

Jack continued smiling so he obviously had got what he went in for. What a trusting soul. Good on him.

```
Name: Ada, hairdresser
Likes: Mike Oldfield, Meatloaf, Skunk Anansie,
       Eric Clapton, Moby
Familiar with Nick Drake's music: No
```

'If it came on the radio I wouldn't turn it off.'

When I came across Keith on the Scottish coast he was on a motorcycling tour. He had just stopped for a break and something to eat. He wasn't aware of Nick Drake and, after listening, told me that although he wouldn't purposely go out and buy the track, if it came on the radio he wouldn't turn it off. Although that may sound like faint praise, he said he often retuned the radio when something came on he didn't rate.

'That's quite good, actually. The music is typical seventies, isn't it?' he observed. 'It's very calming – soothing I would say.' Keith handed the headphones back, got on to his motorbike, and disappeared into the distance, soothed.

```
Name: Keith, conservatory fitter
Likes: Northern soul, Tamla Motown, soul,
    Alicia Keyes
Familiar with Nick Drake's music: No
```

*'How will I remember his name? Oh I know, my son likes ducks.
And Nick, well, I can remember that.'*

```
Name: Janet, chef
Likes: Shania Twain, Celine Dion, Whitney Houston
Familiar with Nick Drake's music: No
```

It was a grey drizzly February day. I was walking uphill and was catching up with the woman in front of me. It wasn't that I was particularly fast, but she happened to be carrying a huge number of cumbersome carrier bags, all full. Oh, and she was walking with crutches.

As I drew level, I offered her some assistance but she said that she could manage. In fact, she was quite insistent. Although I admired her determination and independence, I was not going to let her struggle anymore so I took a couple of bags from her and we walked along together.

It turned out that Janet had just had some bones fused and she admitted that she had been told not to carry any weight. I didn't ask which bones because just the phrase 'bones fused' had me limping and queasy.

I gave her the opportunity to hear the track and she immediately said, 'Oh, go on then.' While she listened, she was interrupted a few times by people driving or walking past waving at her. Each time she pointed at the headphones on her head and mouthed, 'I am listening to something' in the way that Les Dawson used to do when he would utter an unfinished sentence silently, with his lips exaggerating the words. 'That was quite, quite lovely,' Janet told me when the track had ended before disappearing into the charity shop she had been heading to all along.

*'I've heard this song before.
This is alright.
I used to hear this song in a squat.'*

```
Name: John, currently not working
Likes: punk, dub reggae, Clint Eastwood and
       General Saint, ska
Familiar with Nick Drake's music: Yes
```

Some time ago John was the lead singer in a punk band called Aftermath. They played around the north of England, he told me, but they stopped getting bookings 'because there was too much chaos when we played.'

John looked up from the bench he was on after the recording finished and said, 'It's strange. He doesn't sound particularly young at all.'

John thought the track was really good. I had a feeling that he would recognise Nick Drake's music. Although punk rockers railed against the Pomp Rockers like ELP and Pink Floyd, they didn't against some of the more folkie songwriters. I remember John Peel talking about a studio session with John Lydon who, much to his surprise, had turned up with some of his own vinyl collection, including an old favourite copy of John Martyn's Solid Air which, said Peel 'was in perfect condition'.

'It made me want to hum.'

Jasmin sat on a stone on the ground in a field in the Welsh hills and listened as the sun went down one February evening. She told me afterwards that she didn't know if the music was happy or sad but it made her want to hum. Digger the dog seemed to want to get in on the act, as did Jasmin's little sister Alexa. Later on that evening, Jasmin played the euphonium while I played the guitar in a rather surreal little jam session.

```
Name: Jasmin, primary school pupil
Likes: Girls Aloud, Miley Cirus
Familiar with Nick Drake's music: No
```

'It is the sort of thing you drift off to and what a perfect place to listen to it, under an oak tree on a sleepy Sunday.'

```
Name: Seth, musician
Likes: The Avett Brothers, John Butler Trio,
       Stéphane Grappelli and Django Reinhardt
Familiar with Nick Drake's music: Very
```

Seth is unusual among the subjects of the project in that he has worked with Nick Drake's superb sound engineer John Wood, of whom he spoke highly.

He interpreted the different cello sound on the recording as having been achieved by the use of a delay, however, we were in a field with the Cornbury Festival in full swing. Quite nearby The Fishermen's Friends were letting cry in full voice.

'That is rather lovely,' he said. 'All the parts are recognisable and it is great the way that the percussionist reacts to the lyrics. I wonder if that is Nick Drake himself playing the percussion.'

He then disappeared. Ten minutes later he took to the stage and played a really excellent set himself.

Although Seth pressed the headphones closer to his head to hear the track, when I saw this picture later it made me smile. It looks like they could be someone else's hands.

'Let's do it.'

I spotted Dan standing alone on a desolate station in the heart of the Midlands one Wednesday night in March. After stopping the car, I ran across the road and up onto the platform. Dan looked like the sort of young man that the right wing press would have people running from in fear. He was wearing a hooded top and had a black eye.

While I was telling him what I was doing his mobile phone went off, but he got rid of the caller quickly. 'I'm with some guy who wants to take photos of me,' he told them. Ringing off, he turned back to me: 'Sure, let's do it.'

There was a moment when I wondered who ought to be more scared, the middle-aged man alone on a station platform with a hoodie-wearing teenager sporting a black eye or the teenager who had just been approached by a stranger saying, 'Put these headphones on, and listen to some music while I take some photos of you.' I know who my money would be on.

While he was listening, a fast train came through, knocking him off his feet. It must have come as a tremendous shock to Dan, who had his back to it. 'Shit, that was my train,' he said. I didn't understand this comment because it seemed to imply that trains could be hailed, but he stood up, put the headphones back on and continued to listen.

When the song came to the end he came up with the most unexpectedly lovely quote of the entire project: 'well tranquil'. It had looked anything but.

```
Name: Dan, student
Likes: drum and bass
Familiar with Nick Drake's music: No
```

*'Just incredible.
The flourishes on the strings rising up, incredible.
Much more fragile.'*

```
Name: Spencer, music archivist
Likes: punk, psych, indie, rock and folk,
       Nick Drake, Pink Floyd (with Syd)
Familiar with Nick Drake's music: Very
```

Taking this photograph gave me great pleasure. Spencer was so incredibly clued up on every cough, whistle and cluster chord that Nick Drake had ever recorded that he could not contain his excitement at hearing something that he hadn't known existed by an artist he so admired. His first words when he removed the headphones were succinct: 'Fucking hell,' he said with a look of amazement on his face. 'Just incredible.'

Afterwards he looked at his girlfriend, Ruby, and said, 'You really have to listen to that.' I could hardly refuse, especially as Ruby was as keen on Nick Drake's material as Spencer. Then he turned to me and said, 'It sounds claustrophobic in a way. His voice is well recorded and close miked.' We talked a good deal about Nick Drake and, as I handed the headphones to Ruby, he said, 'That was lovely, it is on a par with the home recording of Hazey Jane.' Ruby smiled and looked excited.

'*Quite chilled out. Nice with the sun out and everything.*'

Name: Ashleigh, student of contemporary applied arts
Likes: dub reggae, Dub Syndicate
Familiar with Nick Drake's music: No

Ashleigh and two friends were off for a day's mountain biking. A regular attendee of the Big Chill festival, she thought that if she heard the track there she would sit and listen to hear 'something different'.

One of the questions I asked everybody I photographed was 'what do you do?' I would often hazard a guess at the answer before they told me and frequently I was so far from the reality it was laughable.

Have a look at Ashleigh because she told me that she does something more than just study contemporary applied arts. I have deliberately not put it in the description at the top of this page to give you a chance to have a guess at which of these is the correct answer.

As well as being a student, which of these is true about Ashleigh?

    A) Ashleigh is a drag racer.
    B) Ashleigh has invented and markets a non-toxic variety of nail varnish.
    C) Ashleigh is a high-wire walker.
    D) Ashleigh is an ice sculptor.
          or
    E) Ashleigh deals in, and has the largest collection of, pre-war radios in Britain.

Commiserations to anyone who said B, C, D or E.

'That was alright, mate.'

Ray had positioned himself on the intersection of two roads in west London and was busy restoring the seat of an old chair with reed, his legs intertwined around the legs of the chair, keeping it in position as he weaved away. Fascinated, I went over and asked him if he would like to hear the track. 'No, not now,' he said. So I went shopping. On my way back I asked him again. 'I'm sort of useless when it comes to music,' he told me.

Lying on the pavement was a pile of business cards. As we chatted, a woman came and admired Ray's work. She stooped down, picked up one of the cards, and said, 'I have a couple of wonderful old chairs that need some work. I'll call you.' Ray nodded to her and she walked off but I remained. Ray was obviously getting bored of my presence. 'Oh, go on then.' He motioned towards my rucksack.

I put the headphones on him as he continued his restoration. While he listened and worked, another woman looked over his shoulder admiring his work, then picked up one of the cards. Ray acknowledged her with a nod.

When the track finished, I removed the headphones from Ray's head. 'That was alright mate. It was different but it seems familiar, sort of classical.'

I was intrigued by Ray's idiosyncratic approach to work. 'I come from the other side of the river' he told me. 'My family has been doing this since 1850. A lot of trade comes this way. By working on the roadside I can hand out fifty cards a day.' Brilliant, I thought. I patted him on the back and took one of his cards. He nodded at me.

```
Name: Ray, chair restorer
Likes: Elvis Presley, The Rolling Stones
Familiar with Nick Drake's music: No
```

'It's sad, isn't it? It makes me want to go home and listen to one of his albums. There was a posthumous one, wasn't there? Maybe that one.'

```
Name: Tom, writer
Likes: grandad rock, 'whatever shows up on the
       radio', Arctic Monkeys, Libertines
Familiar with Nick Drake's music: Yes
```

I had never really thought about where Tom Stoppard came from, so his slightly clipped Eastern European accent took me a little by surprise. He was good company and interesting. His last play, he told me, was called Rock and Roll. Syd Barrett's physical and mental decline plays a role in the drama, which ends with a concert by the Rolling Stones.

Tom put on the headphones, lit a cigarette and listened. When the recording finished he asked if I thought that they would keep re-releasing Nick Drake's material over and over again. It was an interesting question for another artist to ask. I'd read that when Joe Boyd, Nick's manager, sold his Witchseason Production company to Island Records in the early 1970s he did so on the condition that Drake's albums would never be deleted. This seems to me like an admirable contractual clause.

Researching Sir Tom after our encounter, I discovered that his father was a doctor at the shoe company Bata in Czechoslovakia. Bata manufactured the Wayfinder, which was the shoe of choice for all nerdy young schoolboys in the 1960s. They had a compass secreted in the inside heel of one shoe and animal footprints on the sole. I own a mint boxed pair from 1969, which are incredibly rare. Had I known about his father earlier, I would have mentioned this when I met him. But now I am doing it here in print. Yup, I own some Wayfinders that I can't get into. Form a queue, girls.

'I cannot believe that that was in the bottom of a skip – that's just mental.'

```
Name: Emily, singer/songwriter
Likes: Louis Jordan, Bach, Bob Marley,
       Tracy Chapman, Suzanne Vega
Familiar with Nick Drake's music: Yes
```

Emily placed the headphones on her head and leaned against the outer wall of the large country estate where I had just watched her perform. Some of her songs had a wondrous sadness to them so I suspected that Nick Drake would be of interest to her. I told her the story of the tape and she was amazed. We talked for a while about writing and Emily told me that she has periods of writer's block but at other times the songs just pour out of her. She was blocked at the moment, but still great company.

As she listened, I watched her eyes moisten in exactly the same way Robert Kirby's (Nick's friend and string arranger) had done when he had heard the recording. 'I feel seriously honoured,' she said when she took the headphones off.

Emily talked about the recording before saying, 'I have always felt a connection with Nick Drake as I have had a lot of darkness in my life and that informs my songs and I am sure it informed his.'

Go see Emily Maguire. She writes a hell of a song. And I wish her light whenever there is darkness.

'I spotted some spiritual stuff in there.'

```
Name: Brendan, tattooist, craftsman
Likes: 'It depends what mood I'm in. I like anything
       that's good.'
Familiar with Nick Drake's music: No
```

The back of Brendan's van had been crafted to look like a castle with wooden turrets and all sorts. I found him sitting drinking coffee inside and he looked as snug as anything on what was a fairly cold evening on the Sussex seafront. I would have put money on Brendan having heard of Nick Drake, but I was wrong.

He positioned himself so he was looking out from his kitchen at the sea, sitting on the bottom half of what looked like stable doors. As the track continued, dogs started to appear. There was something really homely about the inside of the van. I supposed that was because it was a home. Everything had a place and there was a place for everything.

'It's a good tune,' he said, taking off the headphones. 'If he was still alive he would be playing at many a hippy festival. It reminded me a little of Cat Stevens.' I explained that they were stablemates at their record company. 'That figures' he said and commented that it would probably take him a few more listens to appreciate the lyrics. I wondered if that would be true or whether Brendan would be like a lot of other people who listen to Nick Drake and find the lyrics drift uncatchably through their mind like mist as the music transports them somewhere else entirely.

'That's nice chilling-out music to have on in the background and everybody is happy,' Brendan said as I left. I left smiling and happy too.

'It would be lovely background music to have on all the time.'

Name: Shirley, retired riding instructress and lab technician
Likes: Frank Sinatra, Matt Monro
Familiar with Nick Drake's music: No

Shirley and her husband moved up to north east Scotland many years ago, after he had served in the army for 23 years.

They live not far from Pennan, which is where I came across them. Pennan is the stunningly beautiful, isolated village that serves as the fictional village of Ferness in Bill Forsyth's seminal film Local Hero.

Local Hero is possibly the greatest film in the history of mankind and the Locations Manager should be knighted for finding Pennan. It is simply that good.

This was Shirley's first time in Pennan, despite living just down the road for many years. I have lost count of the times I have been to Pennan despite living over 600 miles away. If my first day in Pennan had been accompanied by a lost Nick Drake recording, I might have considered asking the grim reaper to finish it for me there and then, as life wasn't going to get much better.

Thankfully, Shirley loved the recording, loved Pennan, didn't summon the reaper and promised to go and watch Local Hero for the very first time which I was confident she would love. Hence I now love Shirley.

'When I was younger the introspective vocal delivery didn't really grab me, but now I'm old and miserable I get it.'

Name: David, professional broadcaster, amateur guitarist
Likes: Pat Metheny, blues, Arvo Pärt, guitar music
Familiar with Nick Drake's music: Yes

I came across David in Oxford where he had been interviewing Patti Smith at the literary festival in front of an awestruck crowd. I queued politely at the book signing afterwards to see if Patti fancied putting the headphones on. During the interview she had talked about her professional relationship with John Cale and how they had, back in the USA, talked about all things British. Cale is Welsh and Patti, it turns out, has British roots. Their love of certain

British music helped them bond during the time Cale produced Smith's huge selling 70s album Horses. I took this as a sign that Patti would be a big Nick Drake fan because Cale rated Drake's work very highly and had worked with him. He played on Bryter Layter, Drake's second album.

I found myself queuing for over an hour as it turned out that the whole audience wanted a signed copy of her book. From a distance, I watched as she was kind and considerate to all who came to the desk. People asked for advice as though she was a wise guru.

As the queue shortened, I realised that the people towards the end of queues for literary signings tend to be more on the strange side. A women two in front of me offered Patti the keys to her apartment in the States to stay 'any time'. The man directly in front of me pulled six copies of her book (the same book) out of his bag and, I am sure, asked 'Could you sign them all to Richard please.'

Then it was my turn. And how mad was I now going to appear after that? 'Oh, hi Patti,' I said, holding my book out for her to sign to look a bit normal. 'I was just wondering if you would like to be one of the first 200 people to hear a recently discovered recording by Nick Drake.'

She looked at me and, sounding like Bob Dylan with a chest complaint, said perfectly pleasantly, 'I ain't never heard of Nick Drake…gotta go.' And with that she scribbled her name on my opened book and left the marquee. I felt like shouting after her 'Well, I've never heard Horses.' I didn't though. Instead, I sauntered out of the tent into the rain and tripped over in a puddle. Lying there I thought: that is an hour I'm not getting back. What on earth am I doing?

I pulled myself up and walked round the grounds of Christ Church as the rain started to abate and there I came across David looking suitably friendly. 'The lyrics, they're not very happy are they?' he said as the track came to an end. 'I like it now more than when I first heard it as it has a severe lack of minor thirds.'

David, it turned out, was a guitarist, too, and he had played at the legendary folk club Les Cousins, where Drake had played on a number of occasions. He'd seen him too. 'It's alright that track,' he continued. 'It's one of the songs on my wife's shop's playlist.' I shook hands with David and turned to leave Oxford, feeling a little strange and vowing not to target anyone specifically again.

*'His music just weeps.
It is sincere and heart wrenching.'*

I stopped Damian because he was carrying a guitar case. When I asked if he liked Nick Drake, he came back with the answer: 'Of course I like Nick Drake.' It was a splendid response because it has overtones of: what a ridiculous question, doesn't everyone?

Battling with the heavy noise of London traffic, Damian pressed the headphones closer to his ear with his left hand. It was only when I got the photograph home that I noticed that he had unconsciously replicated the pose of Oscar Wilde in the poster behind him.

```
Name: Damian, musician
Likes: Ray LaMontagne, Nick Drake,
       great songwriters
Familiar with Nick Drake's music: Very
```

'There is no violence in his voice at all.'

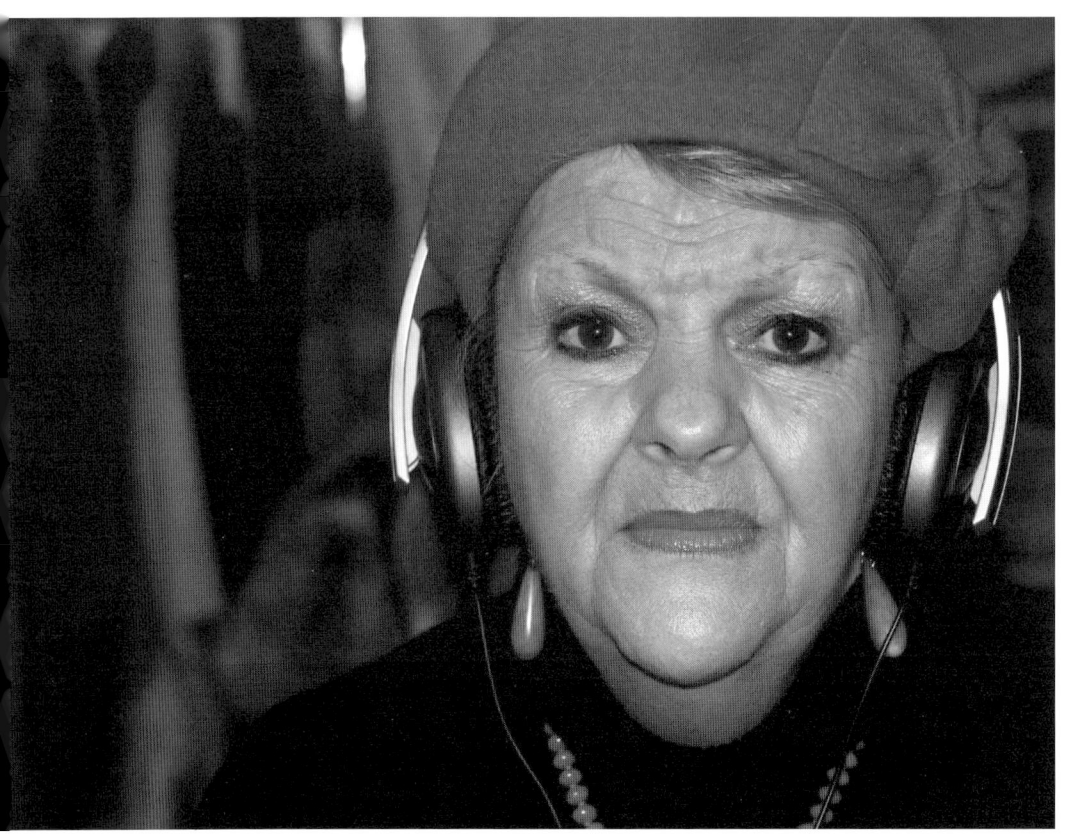

```
Name: Diane, vintage clothing shop owner
Likes: Al Bowlly, Elvis Presley, Noel Coward,
       Pavarotti, Queen, Mark Knopfler
Familiar with Nick Drake's music: No
```

Sometimes, if asked, I would give a potted version of Nick Drake's life story to someone after they had finished listening to the recording. Occasionally, I would tell somebody before. Diane is a sensitive soul and it is obvious to me that she is listening to the track having just taken in Nick's story. I look at this photograph and think that a photographer not only has the ability to record but the ability to affect the end result.

Anyway, back to Diane…Diane is a friend and I have met few more generous people in my life. She can be opinionated though, so here are a few of the things Diane muttered after listening.

'Reminds me of Tom Paxman' (sic). Now that is an edition of Newsnight I would like to see.

'Reminds me of Clifford T Ward'

'Reminds me of Bread'

'I loved it, so gentle, so gentle.'

'It is easy listening, you don't get fed up with people like that. Ella Fitzgerald, Bette Midler, Sarah Vaughan, Billie Holliday, now they can sing.'

'Girls Aloud, can she sing? No she can't.'

'The Maharishi seems very close by.'

I stopped Alan as he was cycling and he agreed to listen in a flash. He parked his bike and we chatted a bit. I showed him some of the photographs I had taken and he was complimentary. I, in turn, complimented him on Cracked Actor, his seminal David Bowie documentary from the 1970s. He told me that the model Kate Moss had also been enthusiastic about it a week or two earlier. We then had a good-spirited name-dropping competition, which he resoundingly won, trumping me by producing a photograph from the previous week on his mobile phone of Island Record's founder Chris Blackwell and Mick Jagger together.

After the track came to an end Alan said, 'I can't take that on my desert island as I've already done that.' When he appeared on the radio show Desert Island Discs, he took tracks by Billie Holliday, Hank Williams, Puccini and Mozart among others but that was over fifteen years ago. I wonder what that list would look like now. Maybe that's an idea… Desert Island Discs Redux, a programme in which people talk about how their musical tastes have changed over the years. It maybe that Alan's tastes haven't changed at all, but the luxury he took on the island was a VHS player and surely he wants to update that.

'This track is all about mood,' he said. 'I like the humming very much.'

I liked our twenty minutes together very much. We shook hands and said goodbye.

```
Name: Alan, TV executive and presenter
Likes: Richard Strauss's four last songs,
       Gorrillaz, The Rolling Stones
Familiar with Nick Drake's music: Yes
```

*'It sounds as if it is a riff that is going to develop
but it just becomes a vehicle for the lyrics, which is engaging.'*

```
Name: Micheál, herald at arms
Likes: Lambert Hendricks and Ross, King Pleasure,
       Dizzy Gillespie
Familiar with Nick Drake's music: No
```

I came across Micheál while he was fishing for grayling on the River Itchen and, I have to say, I found him a total pleasure. As for his musical tastes, it just shows that you can never judge a book by its cover. I would have had him down more as a Bach man. More fool me. A lesson I learned over and over again on my travels was that you cannot guess people's musical preferences with any great accuracy by looking at them, although this didn't stop me trying. His knowledge of bebop was pretty encyclopaedic. He liked the track 'well enough', which I thought was a lovely phrase.

'I hope you don't mind me saying this but it's a little bit depressing. Not my sort of music at all.'

```
Name: Matthew, car mechanic
Likes: The Verve, Oasis, 'a bit of everything'
Familiar with Nick Drake's music: No
```

At last! A man who didn't enjoy the recording. Up until that point most people just seemed to like it, but then Matthew came along. In fact, he came along to mend my car and I gave him the opportunity to put on the headphones. One of the things I said to people who didn't know Drake's music was, 'You won't offend me if you don't like it. Just listen and tell me what you think.' Well, Oasis-loving Matthew listened and told me straight. Good on him.

'I am still trying to process what just happened.'

Everything seemed to be going well until Julian heard the first few bars and exclaimed in an accusatory tone, 'Not *this* one.'

'It is a known track, but an unknown version,' I explained as he started to take the headphones off. Placated, he put them back on and listened attentively.

It was then that I appreciated the amount of trust I was asking people to put in me. Imagine if, having described what they were about to hear, I had given them the headphones and all they heard was a recording of me growling over and over again, 'I like the way you wear your trousers.'

Julian wanted to know if it was the same line up as the released version of Cello Song. While I couldn't accurately say at that point, my suspicion was that it was a different percussionist and that Danny Thompson, the bass player, wasn't on it.

When I asked him what sort of music he liked his comedy partner Noel chipped in with, 'He likes jazz, he really does.' But Barratt struck me as a man who doesn't like to answer such questions without a good deal of contemplation, unlike Howard Moon, the jazz-loving character he plays in The Mighty Boosh. I found Barratt comfortable company. He reminded me very much of an old work colleague of mine. You could only gauge how much he liked a piece of music by the speed at which he stroked his beard.

```
Name: Julian, comedian, actor, musician
Likes: Bartok (especially Bluebeard's Castle),
       Silver Apples
Familiar with Nick Drake's music: Yes
```

'Nice easy listening.'

```
Name: John, butcher
Likes: Wet Wet Wet, Johnny Cash
Familiar with Nick Drake's music: No
```

The phrase easy listening can often be shorthand for bland. I didn't get the impression from John that this was what he meant, but you never know. When John told me that his surname was Smith I said, 'John Smith – you're not having me on, are you?' He looked at me and said, 'My name is a mere nothing compared with my sister, who is quite genuinely called Delia, just like the cookery writer.'

I thanked him for allowing me backstage in a butchers. It was unbelievably clean and the whole shop was really well laid out. I don't know if it is my role to do this but…what the heck. **GO GET YOUR MEAT AT RICKI LLOYDS THE BUTCHERS IN WELSHPOOL, MID WALES. DELIA SMITH DOES**.

'The problem is the way he died. I find him quite difficult to listen to.'

```
Name: Bryan, fish farmer
Likes: Paul Brady, Rolling Stones
Familiar with Nick Drake's music: Yes
```

While on the Scottish coast I took a turning at the foot of some steep hills. The road headed down to the sea and at the bottom I came across what turned out to be a busy salmon farm. Bryan, who worked there, came over and asked if he could help.

I enquired if he knew of Nick Drake and it turned out he had heard Brad Pitt on the Radio 2 documentary about Nick's life and this had led him to buy Nick's albums. 'That's quite a good recording, that' he said at the end of the track. 'Has it been re-mastered?' I explained that it hadn't. 'It is quite timeless. It doesn't sound dated. Not to me, anyway. It's typical Nick Drake, plaintive as usual. I wonder where he would've gone.'

We talked for a while and a fellow worker came over to find out what we were up to. After I'd explained, the co-worker said, 'You should hear Bryan some time.' Bryan had to get back to work so I never got the chance to ask in what way he was musical. However, if it turns out that Bryan is half as musical as he was charming, polite, interesting and engaging, then I suspect he is a virtuoso.

'This is quite good actually.'

```
Name: Robina, customer services manager
Likes: rock
Familiar with Nick Drake's music: No
```

I asked Robina if she would like to hear the track while we both queued at a cash machine in Notting Hill and she replied gamely, 'Oh, go on then.' When I asked her what sort of music she normally liked her response was a vague 'rock, generally'. But she was more forthcoming about what she didn't like. 'Well, I'm not keen on opera, except maybe for La Boheme by Puccini and some of Mozart's work. In fact, I generally like anything that doesn't blow your head off.' I liked this response very much and I told her that I thought she might like Nick Drake. She did as it turned out.

'It's still got that descending cello line going on, and is it faster?'

```
Name: Danny, broadcaster, writer
Likes: numerous including John Martyn,
       Todd Rundgren, Emerson Lake and Palmer,
       Anthony Newley, Steely Dan, Frank Zappa,
       Tommy Steele and The Silver Seas
Familiar with Nick Drake's music: Very
```

I first met Danny Baker in the late seventies when he was starting to write for the NME. The day I photographed him was the first time I had seen him in nearly thirty years. It wasn't this past acquaintance that made him one of the few people I actively approached during this project, but the two-hour show he did on Radio London the day John Martyn died. It was one of the most unlikely but phenomenal bits of broadcasting I have ever cried my way through. The death of John Martyn was like a Princess Diana moment for 'heads' and Danny's raw, honest programme, broadcast live five minutes after he learned of Martyn's death, was a surreal but heartfelt highlight in a brilliant broadcasting career.

He easily spotted all the differences in the recording from the original known version of Cello Song. When I described coming across the tape in a record company skip, he told me that I had just described his idea of heaven.

We chatted briefly and two minutes after listening, he looked at the time and realised that his live radio show had started already. We shook hands and he walked into the studio and got on with his show without missing a beat.

'That's quite nice, that song.'

```
Name: Jon, advertising agency creative director
Likes: AC/DC, Kiss, Alice Cooper, The New York Dolls
Familiar with Nick Drake's music: No
```

As I approached Jon he was listening to Learning English Lesson One by the German punk band Die Toten Hosen (The Dead Trousers), a band who learnt the English language through listening to their favourite British punk bands. It was hard to think that Nick Drake was going to be Jon's kind of thing.

Although I preferred it when people enjoyed the track it didn't bother me too much if they didn't but, I thought, it would be a small victory if Jon ended up liking the recording. So I was secretly pleased when he said, 'That's quite nice, that song.' Rare praise indeed from the Metal-loving joker.

A small victory to Nick Drake, I thought.

'It's got an Asian influence, hasn't it?'

```
Name: Ken, painter
Likes: salsa, rock and roll, country,
       Beuna Vista Social Club
Familiar with Nick Drake's music: No
```

You may be interested to know that this picture features the youngest grandson of the leader of the 1924 Everest expedition on which Mallory and Irvine tragically died.

I came across Ken outside (I imagine you have guessed this) Polbain Stores on the north west coast of Scotland. After ascertaining that I wasn't the tax man, he took off his flat cap, sat on the bench, and got his chance to concentrate on some music. Ken was familiar with Nick Drake by reputation. 'I know of his demise through comments I hear on the radio. He was obviously quite well regarded.' When he took the headphones off, he described the track as being 'quite good and easy'.

Ken likes to concentrate on music, unable to talk to anyone if there is music on in the background, but he has always had a problem with lyrics. When he was younger, he used to have to get his sister to interpret Beatles' lyrics and explain what they meant, even though he is originally from Liverpool.

Just coming back to my first point about the Everest expedition, you might notice that there are two people in the photograph and to anyone who assumed that Ken (on the right) was the grandson of the leader of the 1924 Everest expedition I have to inform you that you are incorrect. Astonishingly, it is actually eight year old Ben, on the left. I think they might breed quite late in that family. I am not sure that many eight year olds these days could say that their grandfather had fought in the First World War.

*'The fact that it was cold and windy
didn't bother me as I just went with the sound.'*

```
Name: Andy, sales manager
Likes: Deep Purple, Genesis, ABC, Duran Duran,
       'but these days more Avenged Sevenfold and
       lostprophets'
Familiar with Nick Drake's music: No
```

I was walking along the Malvern Hills when Andy came into view. As he went through a long list of the metal bands he liked, his wife interrupted by saying: 'You like some of Take That's stuff as well.' I made a note and Andy interrupted. 'If you mention Take That in my list of likes you are going down that hill.' He pointed downwards rather aggressively. I definitely won't mention Take That in his list of likes, I thought.

Putting on the headphones, he pulled some rather striking poses of a windswept man standing on a hill.

'As walking music that would be great,' he said when the track had finished. 'As I would only get a couple of hundred yards through that track.' I took from this that Andy was not as much a fan of walking as his wife Helen. 'That's the sort of thing you could listen to when walking the dog or eating,' he continued. 'I was chillaxed.'

Andy was great company and got the project immediately. He finished up by telling me two things:

1) 'This sounds like James Taylor'
2) 'I [Andy] am handsome.'

I agreed a tiny bit with one of these statements. Oh, and also, Andy likes Take That.

*'I just let Nick Drake's songs wash over me
except for Day is Done when I do concentrate on the lyrics.'*

```
Name: Ottilia, student
Likes: Placebo, Aaron
Familiar with Nick Drake's music: Very
```

In the grounds of a large stately home in the west of England I bumped into Ottilia. Before she could listen to the track, it became obvious that the concert I was there to attend was about to start up and I had to go.

I looked for her after the concert and was disappointed to see that she had gone, but as I was getting into the car she appeared, almost running towards me. Great, I thought, because I hated the idea that I had made somebody the offer to hear the recording and then they didn't get the chance.

She sat down on a large wooden seat by a magnificent old door and put on the headphones, becoming very placid. 'It's incredible to listen to something that so few people have heard and it's really nice listening to the sonorous quality of his voice,' she told me afterwards. But, like many people, she mentioned that Nick Drake's lyrics tend to wash over her.

As a footnote: about six months later I coincidentally saw Ottilia in the Ashmolean Museum in Oxford, which is a hundred or so miles from where this photograph was taken. She remembered the experience with some enthusiasm and commented on its surreal nature. Not as surreal as it feels to see you here, I thought.

'There is a tone under it all of unresolved feeling.'

```
Name: Tracy, writer
Likes: Talking Heads, REM, Elvis Costello,
       Red Hot Chilli Peppers, John Hiatt,
       Lyle Lovett
Familiar with Nick Drake's music: No
```

A few years ago Tracy wrote a book about Nick Drake's favourite poet, William Blake. She was aware of Nick Drake by reputation but was not familiar with his work. Like a number of people, once she had the headphones on, she turned the whole episode into a real-life video, just watching, responding and smiling as birds flew by and people came into view.

I spoke to Tracy a little while after and she told me that later that day, while going through some CDs on a shelf at home, she spotted Pink Moon, Drake's final studio album. No one in the household knew whose it was or where it had come from. It had never been played. It has now.

'It wasn't too heavy, it was just mild.'

Pete was one of a handful of people I photographed who said that they didn't really listen to much music. I had to press him to find out what, if anything, he listened to at all. I loved the way the headphones never came off, despite half a dozen customers buying things from him in the four minutes and twenty two seconds the track took to hear. At the end, Pete said, 'It was alright. It sounds like something to relax to, really.'

Throughout the time he listened, various dogs would suddenly appear from behind the counter in his booth and lean over the top, looking every bit like they worked there. I am sure one customer seeing Pete in the headphones addressed the bigger of the dogs and asked if he had a copy of Vogue, but I might have imagined this.

```
Name: Pete, newspaper vendor
Likes: Irish music and old 60s and 70s stuff
Familiar with Nick Drake's music: No
```

'I liked the lyrics. They were dreamy.'

```
Name: Frances, retired teacher
Likes: religious and choral music
Familiar with Nick Drake's music: No
```

Sometimes on my tour round Britain, I felt a bit like Lobby Lud, who used to walk around seaside resorts in the 1930s on behalf of the News Chronicle, handing out a 10 pound note to the first two people to correctly challenge him. I met up with Frances in the Midlands. She walked around as she listened to the track and I kept out of her way, taking the occasional shot from a distance, though I could hear the gentlest tuneful humming. She looked really happy. Eventually she took the headphones off. 'I loved it' she said. 'It was classical folksy.'

It was moments like this that made me feel really happy. 'What was your name?' she asked.

'Michael' I said. I thought Lobby, though.

'I would never have thought this was that old.
The music is wonderful, it sort of washes over you.'

Name: James, stonewaller
Likes: Scottish folk, punk such as Fugazi,
    Radiohead
Familiar with Nick Drake's music: No

My car was playing up, so I stayed overnight with some friends in the small Somerset village of Chew Stoke, borrowed a car from them the next day, and drove slowly to the north west of Scotland, just short of Cape Wrath – a distance of some 620 miles in all.

After having slept in an old cottage overlooking the sea, I sauntered down to the shorefront feeling refreshed and happy. After a while, I decided to explore a bit more and drove down some narrow mountain roads until I saw a chap standing by the top of a long driveway in a pretty remote area. Introducing myself, I told him what I was up to and we began to talk.

It turned out that he was a stone-waller called James. With his six months old daughter, Florence, he was waiting for his father-in-law to arrive. I commented on James's lack of a Scottish accent and he explained that he had moved up from England some time ago.

'Whereabouts did you come from?' I asked.

'Somerset.'

'Where in Somerset?'

'A small village. You probably won't know it.'

'Try me,' I said, but I think deep down I already knew what he was going to say.

'Chew Stoke.'

'Wow, ain't that a thing. That's where I've driven from.'

I do love a tidy coincidence and James thought it was entirely bizarre.

Finally, he put on the headphones. 'Beautiful and calming,' he observed, before asking which Nick Drake recordings I would recommend he should buy.

'Start with Five Leaves Left and work forward. It'll make you sad, though, as the ending – Pink Moon – isn't happy,' I said.

'Then maybe I should start with Pink Moon and work the other way,'

'Now that's not a bad idea,' I said.

Name: Adrian, artist
Likes: Satie, Puccini, Chopin, Chuck Berry, The Who, John Coltrane, Leonard Cohen, Dinah Washington, Wagner, Mozart, Otis Redding, The Ronettes
Familiar with Nick Drake's music: Hard to tell

'I remember playing poker dice with Nick Drake.'

Occasionally a real surprise would come along, and Adrian was one of them.

When I asked if I could take his photograph for a book, he replied that I couldn't.

'But,' I said. 'You look great with your hat and everything.'

'What is this book?' He almost looked interested.

I explained that it was going to contain photographs of people listening to a long-lost recording by Nick Drake.

'That's a coincidence,' he said. 'Because I knew him. In fact, I remember playing poker dice with Nick Drake back in the sixties.' Then he explained that he was an artist and had been commissioned by Joe Boyd (Nick's manager) to do some artwork for another of Boyd's acts.

I asked Adrian what his full name was and he told me that it was Adrian George.

'So are you a famous artist, Adrian?' I asked.

A big smile came over his face. 'Apparently not,' he replied with great withering comic timing.

I wondered how well Adrian knew Nick Drake's music and he replied 'We used to spend long evenings playing poker dice in a Baudelairean haze. Did he make music as well?'

By this time we had walked for quite a while and he explained how Drake, John Martyn and a host of others would hang out at a drug-filled flat near Ladbroke Grove and, in all-night poker sessions, lose their money to the guy who lived there.

Drake would generally be sitting in a chair in the corner stoned, and everybody who came through thought he was sweet. He would occasionally make up the numbers at the poker table if they were short. 'Nick Drake was not your natural poker player,' Adrian added. With that we drew level to the old gates of The Royal College of Art where Adrian had studied way back. 'Oh sod it, give me those headphones, then, and get your camera out,' he said.

'That was a much more pleasurable experience than I was expecting.'

Name: Don, artist
Likes: Nick Cave, The Fall, rockabilly, psychobilly
Familiar with Nick Drake's music: No

Don owns over 4,000 CDs and 2,500 vinyl albums but had never heard of Nick Drake. When he took the headphones off he said, 'Listening to that made me think of John Martyn.' I had assumed that if you hadn't heard of Nick Drake it was unlikely that you had heard of John Martyn, but seemingly not so.

I explained that Martyn's song Solid Air was written as a tribute to Drake. The tuning of the guitar in Cello Song is not a tuning that Martyn used and their song structures are different but something about the two styles meshed for Don, which was interesting and probably very astute. Slowly, as we spoke about Drake, something about his story started to ring bells and he began to realise that he knew more than he had thought. 'It was more upbeat than I was expecting, too,' he observed. 'It had a good full sound as well.'

We talked more about music and Don revealed that his favourite album was Surfer Rosa by The Pixies, which he said he could listen to forever. I took heed of what Don had said and went home and listened to Surfer Rosa. But not forever.

'I liked the fact that the instrumentation was simple. Fantastic guitar playing and a mellow tone to his voice.'

```
Name: Chris, chaplain
Likes: classic rock, sacred music, Bach
Familiar with Nick Drake's music: No
```

Chris had not heard of Nick Drake before I approached him. He is a chaplain at Trinity College in Cambridge and we were standing on a street that would have been very familiar to Drake, within yards of where he had played live as a student.

Trinity's current choir has been voted the fifth best choir in the world by Gramophone Magazine, which can't be bad for a bunch of undergraduates. Chris was enthusiastic about the recording and in particular Nick's guitar technique.

For a moment after I took this shot I imagined what it might be like if there were such a thing as the afterlife. What a bizarre scene this would be for Nick Drake to look down on: a man of the cloth listening to one of his unreleased recordings from some forty years earlier, while a bumbling fool struggled to take photographs with a new camera that he so patently didn't quite yet fully understand.

'He felt that nobody really appreciated his talent and that's sad for his family as well.'

```
Name: Helen, pianist
Likes: Neil Young, Nick Drake, Mozart, Bach,
       The  Eagles, Bob Dylan, Jackson Browne,
       Claude Bolling, Jacques Loussier
Familiar with Nick Drake's music: Very
```

Helen probably had as much reason to be moved as anyone who donned the headphones. Not only was she a huge fan of Nick Drake, but she lost her brother when he was nineteen. He, too, was a composer and a brilliant musician.

I found that I was not the person for the job of photographing Helen, because there was a lot of movement in her listening procedure. Tears started to build up and I clicked away. But all that happened was both Helen and I began to howl with laughter and I ended up with some blurred photographs. It looked like she was on a fantastic emotional rush and I was delighted that as the track came to an end Helen took off the headphones and said 'that was a very nice experience'. I told her that is was a very nice experience to have shared four minutes and twenty two emotionally charged seconds with her, too.

'I am amazed he is not better known. It's cool.'

Bernard Holley should be carried shoulder-high round the streets of Britain for he holds a remarkable position in the world of entertainment. He is mentioned in Kenneth Williams' diaries half a dozen times and every entry is wholly complimentary, which, if you have read the sometimes hilarious vitriol Williams was capable of pouring on most people he worked with, sets Bernard apart.

Bernard had never heard of Nick Drake. He settled down in his favourite armchair and put the headphones on. He doesn't listen to a great deal of music, but he listened intently to this. 'What a lovely song. I must listen to a bit more,' he told me.

When I was a boy I used to watch Bernard in Z Cars, and he, Andy Williams and Brian Cant were the three men I used to see on television who I wouldn't have minded being my dad. Here I was many years later teasing one of them about the price sticker left on the sole of his favourite slippers. Life is funny like that sometimes.

```
Name: Bernard, actor
Likes: 'I tend to listen to mellow relaxed radio
       music.'
Familiar with Nick Drake's music: No
```

'I think he were born sad.'

In a darkened churchyard in south Yorkshire, Kathryn pulled on the headphones. She knew Nick Drake's material but couldn't immediately summon up the track she was about to hear. 'I'm not good at titles,' she admitted. However, as the song started, a look of recognition came across her face and she pushed the headphones on tighter to get rid of the car noises that occasionally broke the silence.

Rather eerily, an owl flitted across the sky behind Kathryn and I tried to photograph it. I didn't manage it, though, for Eric Hosking I am not.

Maybe it was the location, maybe it was the cold, but when Kathryn took off the headphones she said, 'That's sad. I like that track. It seems sadder than the version I know. I think he were born sad.'

'I was thinking who he might have recorded it for,' she continued. 'It is like he is singing about someone and how they make him feel.' Then she summed up simply and succinctly what so many headphone wearers had tried to describe: 'You get lost in his voice. It is like …' she hesitated. 'A hypnotic voice.'

```
Name: Kathryn, beauty therapist
Likes: Pink, Bruce Springsteen (for the saxophone
       player)
Familiar with Nick Drake's music: Yes
```

'They say the good die young. That is probably why I am still here.'

```
Name: Duncan, musician
Likes: Joni Mitchell, Tony Mcmanus,
       Stefan Grossman
Familiar with Nick Drake's music: Yes
```

It was Duncan's 60th birthday and he was playing traditional and contemporary Scottish music at an incredibly noisy public house on the banks of The River Spey in Aviemore in the highlands of Scotland. I caught him during a break from singing and playing the guitar.

Standing by the river smoking, Duncan pulled on the headphones. He was a hummer and he sort of semi-whistled along with the track, which I rather enjoyed.

He held the CD player very much like you would a discus and I was taken by how much, especially with the cigarette, like a bizarre alternative Highland Olympics it all looked. Afterwards he admitted that he had been tempted to throw it.

'It's amazing what you can do with two chords,' Duncan said when the track had finished. Far from being a dismissive statement, he was full of admiration. 'I haven't heard him for ages. It is right out of that Bert Jansch, Pentangle, Incredible String Band period. That was excellent; a good Nick Drake track.'

I went back in to watch Duncan start up the second half of his birthday gig. The talking was incredibly loud in the bar, but rather than finding this disheartening Duncan just cranked his lungs up a notch and slowly the audience started to quieten.

Happy birthday, Duncan, I sang as I left.

'That was a very moving experience.
Nick Drake has a lot of velvet in his voice.'

```
Name: Melvin, factory worker
Likes: Led Zeppelin, Cream, Pink Floyd, Thunder,
    folk
Familiar with Nick Drake's music: Very
```

Melvin was looking at his father's grave when I went up to him. I wasn't to know that, otherwise I probably wouldn't have approached him at all. We started talking and the conversation eventually moved to music and to Nick Drake. Melvin was aware of Nick Drake's material right from the start because he had sampler albums that had Drake tracks on. I suspect that he was talking about Bumpers, El Pea and Nice Enough To Eat, which were three compilations brought out by Island Records in the late sixties and early seventies. Melvin told me that he liked the songs as soon as he heard them but remained unaware of Drake's death until a few years after the event. 'He died without me noticing,' he said.

The tree, which is one of the largest in the United Kingdom – certainly over seven hundred years old – is a yew. It stands in the churchyard at Much Marcle, Herefordshire. Melvin barely moved a muscle all the time he listened to the track. Afterwards he commented on the surreal nature of what just happened and told me that he had been sitting in a tree where both his late father and grandfather had done their courting. I asked if he had done any courting under the tree. 'No,' he replied, rather quickly.

'I really enjoyed that. It was calming, nostalgic.
I used to know his sister.'

Name: Jonathan, actor
Likes: Beirut, Esbjörn Svensson Trio, jazz
Familiar with Nick Drake's music: Yes

I met Jonathan coming out of a shop in the West End of London. He told me that he had recently been doing The Caretaker. 'Pinter?' I asked. 'Yes,' he said. I realised that 'Pinter?' was a fairly naff response but I still felt secretly pleased with myself.

I really should have paid more attention at school.

Jonathan used to know Gabrielle, Nick Drake's sister, and had his liking for Drake's music re-ignited when his eldest son discovered it back in the 1990s.

Despite becoming momentarily distracted by a pigeon, he listened intently, appearing to genuinely enjoy the strange little break in his day. He seemed pretty knowledgeable about many styles of music and told me about Devandra Banhart, who, in his opinion, follows in Drake's footsteps.

'The guitar and humming were effortless.
You could tell that he was smiling as he played.'

```
Name: Andrew, yoga instructor
Likes: Depeche Mode, Toto, Larry Carlton
Familiar with Nick Drake's music: No
```

Andrew was in this position when I chanced upon him in Holland Park in London. I waited patiently out of his vision until he unfurled himself.

'Was that a crab you were doing?' I asked.

'No, a wheel,' he replied.

At this point I thought that maybe I should ask, 'Can I sit on your tummy and ride you around for Nick Drake's sake?' but unless Andrew knew that Drake had recorded a song called Rider On The Wheel it was a line that was going to fall flat. Thankfully, I didn't say it because Andrew had not heard of Nick Drake.

He put on the headphones and sat cross-legged, then very slowly he put himself back into the wheel position. As I photographed him, I became aware of an empty look in his eyes. I asked him about it when the track had finished. 'While my body and mind are conversing, my being is gone,' he told me. Phew, I thought.

'I need to listen to it a number of times.'

After she heard the track, Danielle explained that she would need to hear it a number of times to be able to pass judgment on it. 'I didn't manage to focus on all the words as you get distracted by all that is going on.'

She gets distracted by all that is going on? Had she seen the room we were sitting in? Plenty going on in here, I thought.

I have known Danielle and her husband, Andrew, for many years and this photo was taken in her parents' back room in Powys, with the splendid portrait of her mother looking down on us both. At Danielle and Andrew's wedding the guests arrived at the beautifully festooned marquee perched on top of a hill in the most wonderful part of Wales to specially chosen music. I distinctly remember that as I entered the marquee Nick Drake's Northern Sky was playing.

```
Name: Danielle, youth worker
Likes: 80s music, soul, reggae,
       Kings of Leon type bands
Familiar with Nick Drake's music: Yes
```

'Quite peaceful. I was paying more attention to the music than the words. There are cellos underneath, which makes it more esoteric, but I would say it is folk.'

```
Name: Mauro, tattoo artist and musician
Likes: punk rock, new wave, metal, psychobilly,
       country
Familiar with Nick Drake's music: No
```

Mauro was standing talking to a couple of friends in a Soho alleyway where he tattoos people. I mean…that is where his parlour is. The world carried on walking past him as he listened but he acknowledged most passers-by with a nod, a wave or an appreciative smile. Everybody seemed to know Mauro.

He was really enthusiastic about the recording and we discussed many forms of music. The punk scene in the west end of London in the 1970s really interested him, although it was before his time. I wished that I could have whisked him back to Dryden Chambers in 1976 and shown him the offices where I remember getting my first copy of Sniffin' Glue. But whereas I purchased the fanzine and vamooshed down the metal external staircase as fast as I could in my big flared trousers past all the assembled punks, Mauro, I'm sure, would have felt much at home there.

'I don't know him. It was just perfect.'

```
Name: Talita, craniosacral therapist
Likes: Abba, Florence and the Machine, Sundays,
       Eat, Neil Diamond, Dolly Parton.
Familiar with Nick Drake's music: No
```

Talita was sitting in a Scottish pub garden with a friend when I approached her. Looking out across the bay at Achiltibuie, she seemed to be a picture of contentment as she listened. Even when a couple of other friends emerged from the pub she remained focused and undistracted. 'That was just such a beautiful song and with this view…perfect. Thank you,' she said warmly.

The next day I was fishing for trout on a small loch nearby and got caught in torrential rain. One of Talita's friends appeared from the other side of the loch, where he had also been fishing. As he ran for the shelter, he told me that Talita had been fishing earlier and had caught her first ever trout on a fly. So, all in all, Talita had experienced two perfect moments in just two short days.

'Any newly discovered Nick Drake recording has to be good for the health of the planet.'

```
Name: Manuel, vinyl record shop proprietor
Likes: Grateful Dead, Neil Young
Familiar with Nick Drake's music: Very
```

Manny runs Rough Trade Vintage record shop just off the Portobello Road and has been really encouraging and supportive of this project. In the photograph he has in front of him a rare copy of the first pressing of Nick Drake's Five Leaves Left from 1969, the album that starts side two with Cello Song. It is on Island Record's early pink label and is the holy grail for many Drake collectors, a single copy selling for many hundreds of pounds. However, Manny tells me that the version to own from a sound perspective is the second pressing which, for him, has more clarity.

When I asked him what music he liked, he replied 'I like all the usual suspects for a man of my age, including Nick Drake.' Go to Manny's shop and buy things. Learn to love vinyl again and remember what it was like to have to put some effort in to listening to your favourite artists as you moved the album sleeve from your lap, placed it onto the floor, staggered over and took the album off the spindle, turned it, blew across the surface and replaced it on the deck and, using the lever on the right hand side, lowered the needle perfectly as the curiously satisfying fizzing, clicking and popping started just before the music.

'Really good and relevant.'

Name: Adam, art student
Likes: Brian Eno
Familiar with Nick Drake's music: No

If you are an art student and habitually dress up as a character in Where's Wally?, what do you think might be the phrase you have to get used to hearing from strangers?

    a) 'I've found you.'

or

    b) 'Would you like to hear an unreleased recording by Nick Drake while I photograph you?'

The answer is of course a, but I decided to give Adam a break by saying b instead.

I wanted to applaud Adam. He is living a bold reality in an unreal world.

'I would suggest that this was a cellist friend who came in and did it on the day. It doesn't sound like a written arrangement.'

```
Name: Richard, arranger, songwriter, producer
Likes: Stravinsky, Bill Evans, Jim Hall,
       Swedish House Mafia
Familiar with Nick Drake's music: Not really
```

Richard Hewson's name may be familiar to Nick Drake fans. Before the sessions at Sound Techniques that resulted in Five Leaves Left, there were some early recordings including Richard Hewson arrangements. When these were rejected, the door was open for Drake's university friend Robert Kirby and Harry Robinson to step in.

It had been suggested that the version of Cello Song I had rescued was a Hewson arrangement, so I decided there was really only one way to find out. What would Richard have to say? I wondered.

I met up with him at his home in Sussex and he turned out to be a real joy: hospitable, informative, funny and kind. He told me it was not a song he recognised, hence not a Richard Hewson arrangement at all. That out of the way, we discussed his memories of Nick Drake.

'I don't think I ever met him,' he said. 'The sixties and seventies were such a busy time for me that it was absolutely non-stop.'

Part of the process of getting music right is sometimes getting it wrong and Hewson's arrangements of Nick Drake's material back then, although not right for Drake, are not bad. Not bad at all. They were just not what was required.

Hewson started off as a guitarist and he was complimentary about Drake's performance on this version of Cello Song. 'He keeps the whole track going with his very accurate guitar playing.' He then asked a question that had cropped up a number of times on my journeys.

'It has an Indian influence. There's a cello run in an Indian raga-like scale, which is not the sort of thing that is ever written down. I wonder which came first, the cello or the voice?'

This was the first time I had really thought about this because on the released version the cello acts in a call-and-response manner but on this unreleased version Drake puts himself with the cellos occasionally singing the same line as they are playing. On the later version, it has been paired down.

Maybe there is still a cellist out there who knows what came first. But as Joe Boyd has no memory of the session, John Wood remembers the guitar and vocals but does not recall recording a cellist on it, Richard Hewson didn't arrange it, and the musicians on the released version didn't play on it, the recording's genesis becomes more shrouded in mystery. However, it remains a wonderful, historic piece of abandoned music and maybe that's all that actually matters.

Hewson continues to write dance music and, just in case you felt the tiniest bit sorry for him because some of his arrangements didn't get used over forty years ago on some Nick Drake recordings, the following is a list of some of the artists whose work his arrangements have adorned: The Bee Gees, James Taylor, Herbie Hancock, Clifford T Ward, Supertramp, Diana Ross, Carly Simon, Art Garfunkel, Mary Hopkin, Al Stewart, Fleetwood Mac and Chris Rea.

Oh, and The Beatles.

Jesse – *'He sings like he's in the cold of the night, to quote one of his lyrics.'*

Fearne – *'I love his voice. It's so haunting.'*

```
Name: Jesse, model/photographer
Name: Fearne, DJ and presenter
Jesse likes: Led Zeppelin and The Smiths
Fearne likes: The Stone Roses, Led Zeppelin,
     David Bowie
Familiar with Nick Drake's music: Yes/Yes
```

Jesse is a photographer and whenever I found myself taking a photograph of a photographer I had to up my game and look as if I knew what I was doing. I am sure these two are photographed a lot but they were charming and Jesse was interested in the project. They both knew of Nick Drake and his work.

When I realised that I went to the same school as Fearne (although its name had been changed and I left a long time before she joined) I desperately fished around in my memory for a teacher who taught long enough to have spanned both of our times there, just to make me appear younger. Thank the lord for John Hawley, the geography master who Fearne remembered.

By my reckoning that means John Hawley was about 129 years old when Fearne was at the school.

Mind you, maths was never my strong point.

Neither was geography come to that.

'Toe-tapping relaxing stuff. Interesting lyrics.'

```
Name: John, retired doctor, lecturer
Likes: classical (especially Edward Elgar),
       trad jazz
Familiar with Nick Drake's music: No
```

John was one of a number of people who expressed astonishment at the fact that they had been listening to a twenty one year old (at most) singing. 'He sounds older than his years,' he observed.

I offered John the headphones when he was walking in the Malvern Hills. He has a real passion for Malvern, having helped set up the museum there. He regularly lectures on its development from village to a popular hydrotherapy spa. I was lucky enough to attend one of his talks about the Victorian water cure but this particular getting-better lark sounded like a wet, cold and generally miserable experience. Eventually people started to rely more on modern medicine and the spas fell into disrepair. Malvern, it would appear, is now a centre for galloping horses, parascending, and men brandishing headphones.

'I don't listen to Nick Drake so I don't know his material.'

```
Name: Ashley, public house landlord
Likes: David Bowie, Northern soul
Familiar with Nick Drake's music: No
```

I walked into The Bell public house in Tanworth in Arden and engaged with a number of customers on the subject of Nick Drake. The Drake family house is just down the road and Tanworth in Arden is the village where Nick grew up, died and is buried. Over the years there has been a constant stream of people (mainly young) from all over the world who have come to pay their respects. They are referred to by the residents as 'Drakies' and although some local people embrace and celebrate their famous son I got the impression that to some in this quiet little Midlands village it is a bit of an inconvenience.

Although The Bell has a nice display of photographs of Nick and a fragment of his multi-coloured poncho in a frame, I was amazed to find that although Ashley the landlord was himself very positive about Drakies he was not familiar with the material. I suppose I had expected to walk in to the Drake family's local pub and hear Pink Moon playing on the music system but, of course, the reality is that non-stop Nick Drake in a pub might be a little bit challenging.

'That was very good actually, you could get that on Chill FM,' Ashley said after he had listened. 'You should go down to the vicarage and ask Paul the vicar if he would like to hear it. It's his day off and he's been busy, but you never know. He is very supportive about Nick Drake and his place in the history of the village.'

'Good idea,' I said, but I had spotted my next headphone wearer already. In fact, maybe you, dear reader, can spot her too.

*'He hasn't bastardised the English language.
It's not mournful like his other stuff.'*

```
Name: Diana, retired
Likes: choral music, The Rolling Stones
Familiar with Nick Drake's music: A bit
```

Diana has tended her husband's grave in the same churchyard where Nick Drake is buried for over fourteen years. She knows that one day she will join her husband there. 'It's not a bad place to be dead,' she told me.

Gentle and friendly, like most people who have been in the village a while, she knew Nick's parents. She had heard his material over the years and although not overly keen on it she was happy to get the chance to listen, having accidentally gate-crashed Ashley the pub landlord's photograph earlier when she asked us what we were up to.

Once upon a time, she told me, she used to sing in a choir and was full of praise for Nick's diction. 'He doesn't sing with estuary speak,' she remarked, something that seemed to please her greatly. 'It has a lovely, lovely backing too.'

Afterwards Diana and I wandered through the graveyard and she showed me Nick's grave, which was surrounded by some new and some wilting flowers and a selection of plectrums and mouth organs placed in tribute in a large pot. Then she left me there and continued on her way to tend her husband's resting place.

'The song felt like mid-afternoon sun on your back.'

```
Name: Jack, student
Likes: David Bowie, The Ramones,
       The Rolling Stones, The Clash
Familiar with Nick Drake's music: No
```

Jack sat on the steps of a Wardour Street office with his feet on the pavement as the world hurried past him at a furious pace.

After he finished listening, his thoughts were seemingly at odds with everything around him. 'I thought it was really mellow and soft and it flowed the way water would flow down a shallow stream over boulders and rocks,' he said. 'It did so much with so little instruments.'

Jack introduced me to lyrical thoughts while stuck in a busy city environment.

For my part, I was really delighted to have introduced Jack to Nick Drake's music.

*'There is something unlearned about it.
It is so quintessentially English.
It's – it's innocent.'*

```
Name: Janet, writer, broadcaster
Likes: classic musicals (Oklahoma, West Side Story),
    Simon and Garfunkel,
    Wilco and the Jayhawks, The Magnetic Fields
Familiar with Nick Drake's music: A bit
```

I had recently watched a documentary on BBC4 celebrating the 30th anniversary of the release of the book Masquerade. Masquerade was a wonderful picture book created by the artist Kit Williams. Within it were the clues to the whereabouts of a buried bejewelled golden necklace in the shape of a hare. Incidentally, it was also the book that took me and some friends to Cornwall with a metal detector where we managed to unearth not a golden hare but a Second World War bomb. Anyway, the documentary was covered in Nick Drake's music and was voiced by Janet Ellis.

Like a number of people, as she began to listen, Janet's eyes slowly moved heavenwards. 'It felt like a very short song,' she remarked when she removed the headphones. 'There is something about being separated from the reality around me that heightened my senses and made it all buzzy and hyper-real. I was listening hard and that, coupled with the images around me, made it feel very filmic.'

I was secretly delighted when she added, 'It is so quintessentially English.' I had been thinking of Englishness while I watched that documentary with Kit Williams, Janet Ellis and Nick Drake together. In fact, I doubt you could find a more quintessentially English trio.

'There is an intangible connection to humanity about this recording.'

```
Name: Elliott, musician
Likes: Stan Getz, George Gershwin, Jimi Hendrix
Familiar with Nick Drake's music: A bit
```

Elliott Randall was one of a handful of people I actively contacted to be part of this project. We met up on a Saturday afternoon in Soho, neither of us realising that it was Gay Pride that day and that the streets would be alive with whistles, singing and shouting. Against the odds, we found a relatively quiet spot. You will have heard Elliott's work more times than you realise and I was intrigued as to what he would make of the experience as many excellent players find it easy to be cynical about other musicians' recordings. Elliott, who was born the year before Nick Drake, has performed with an astonishing array of artists, from The Doobie Brothers to Carly Simon, and his guitar solo on Steely Dan's Reelin In The Years is cited by Jimmy Page as his favourite solo of all time. On top of that he was a good friend of Jimi Hendrix.

I had been clicking away for a couple of minutes, when I thought, oh my goodness, is Elliott crying? I continued to take photos until he eventually removed the headphones.

'Jesus fucking Christ,' he said. 'I was almost in tears for a moment.' I asked what he had thought of the recording. 'I was in another world. Sure, I could hear the crowd noise that was going on around me, but I was completely captured by what was coming through the headphones,' he told me. 'There is something about Nick Drake, Tim Hardin and Tim Buckley's over-sensitivity that may contribute to why we don't have them here any more.'

Elliott is one of the music industry's nice guys. There was no cynicism to anything he said. What I found really positive was that he is still a real fan of other people's music, despite being one of the unsung greats himself.

'That's great.'

```
Name: Alexander, student
Likes: The Jam, The Cure
Familiar with Nick Drake's music: No
```

Alexander was already listening to something on his iPod when I offered him the opportunity to listen. He asked if it would be alright if he used his own headphones, which were in-ear. It was only at this point that I realised how important continuity was for my project. The headphones were just some I had found hanging around at home and thought would be up to the job but they had been a continuous thread through the photos.

In the end, Alexander was absolutely happy to use mine. I wasn't sure what we would do with his hat until he took the headphones from me and put them straight over the top of it. Despite his peculiar listening strategy, he seemed to enjoy the track. Maybe the headgear worked as a kind of noise-reduction system, taking out some of the hissy top frequencies.

'The cellos sound a bit cheeky, quite dark. And then I started to think: what came first the humming or the cello line?'

```
Name: Ruby, Foley artist
Likes: The Beatles, Fairport Convention,
       David Bowie ('of course')
Familiar with Nick Drake's music: Very
```

Ruby knows Drake's material well. The first words that came out of her mouth when removing the headphones a few seconds after this shot were 'wow, amazing'.
She was struck by the situation of standing in the street listening. 'It's not what you do.'

As she gathered her thoughts, she told me that she found the version quite dark. 'But then, there are little chord progressions that are like a sunburst. It is quite beautiful.'

When she told me that she was a Foley artist I mentioned the name of the only Foley artist I had ever met and, of course, it turns out she works with him. In the world of Strange Face, it seems life's like that.

*'You don't see suicide in people's looks.
You never know with some people.'*

Name: Lau Lau, art student
Likes: ambient, electronica
Familiar with Nick Drake's music: No

Lau Lau had not heard of Nick Drake but enjoyed the recording a lot while his three companions stood in the background photographing what was happening.

Occasionally I would be taken by certain phrases people used to describe the track and Lau Lau came up with a word that no-one else uttered on my travels.

'I loved it,' he said. 'It was very easy and…and comfortable.'

Comfortable. I liked that a lot.

'To have such a good voice at that young age. That's amazing.'

```
Name: Jasmin, chip shop manageress
Likes: Dave Edmunds, Foo Fighters, gothic,
    Sean Paul, Eminem, heavy rock.
    'I love all music except for bagpipes.'
Familiar with Nick Drake's music: No
```

Standing outside some public toilets in Wester Ross, I met up with Jasmin. As locations go it felt like a strange place to introduce someone to Nick Drake but Jasmin smiled and was very engaging so we got chatting. I told her a bit about Nick Drake before she put on the headphones. 'Jees-us,' she said after the track finished, 'that is an older voice. A really rich voice. He sounds a bit like Leonard Cohen but actually more like Jeff Buckley. Buckley was better than Cohen.'

We chatted a bit more and Jasmin showed good musical knowledge and I was really taken by her saying how much she liked Dave Edmunds. It was not a name I necessarily imagined was going to crop up much on my travels but it was nice to hear. I loved Jasmin's assertion that she liked all music except for the bagpipes and I told her that I had a weak spot for them because of my Scottish roots and my Grandmother's love of them. On the other hand, I had recently been given the definition of a true gentleman. 'What's that?' asked Jasmin. 'A man who can play the bagpipes… but doesn't,' I replied.

Jasmin returned to the Drake track. 'It's the sort of music you would be sitting with a glass of wine just chilling to,' she said. This image cropped up so often on my travels that I wonder if record shops are missing a category: music to sit and drink to.

'That was very nice. Very, very nice indeed.'

```
Name: Richard, actor and director
Likes: Mozart, Mahler, Aretha Franklin,
       Mumford and Sons, English bluegrass,
       'in fact, most things other than heavy metal'
Familiar with Nick Drake's music: Yes
```

Richard agreed to put the headphones on immediately. 'Let's do it,' he said. He was personable and, it turns out, a huge fan of Masterchef, a TV show I have been involved with.

He likes Nick Drake's material a lot but possibly didn't know Cello Song well enough to be able to spot the differences in the versions. Although he listened quite contentedly, with a minute of the recording still to go, he took off the headphones. I suspected he needed to go.

When I got home and looked at the photographs I became interested in this final one, which was just five seconds before he removed the headphones. To me he looks like a man who had been affected by the recording.

I know Grant is an actor who can summon tears at the drop of a hat but I still find this picture quite moving and it is certainly unlike all the others I took of him.

'It sounded like a traditional Indian song that I would have listened to as a child.'

```
Name: Rashidah, law student
Likes: Mozart, opera
Familiar with Nick Drake's music: No
```

'You don't have this kind of experience every day,' said Rashida after I approached her in Cambridge. She leaned against a pillar outside what was, once upon a time, Robert Kirby's lodgings when he was a student there. This was a house Nick Drake knew very well.

Initially, I had asked Rashida what sort of music she listened to. 'Mozart and opera,' she said. She went on to tell me about her Malaysian background. 'Sometimes I get homesick so I listen to the sort of music my parents used to listen to.'

'So what sort of music did your parents listen to then?' I asked.

'Oh, you know, Elton John, The Beatles – that sort of thing.'

'At first I listened to the lyrics and then the humming distracted me,' Rashida told me after the track finished. Maybe, I thought, that is what Drake does. He takes you off on one route and then, like a pickpocket, distracts you with some humming or a flourish on the guitar which was why I could not retain any of his lyrics in full. 'It sounds a bit oriental. Was that its intention?' Rashida went on. There is no doubt that Davy Graham and others whose music Drake knew would experiment with neutral Indian scales and variations from round the world, so I tried this as an answer. I reckoned I sounded pretty bright. Mind you, Rashida was the Cambridge law student and I was a scruffy oik taking photographs of strangers. I think we know who was the bright one here.

'It's not something I would go and see a gig of.'

```
Name: John, horticulturalist
Likes: Iron Maiden
Familiar with Nick Drake's music: No
```

John was brilliant. Brilliant company, brilliantly informative, brilliantly funny and brilliantly hard of hearing. I came across him at a rugby match and gave him the headphones. 'I can't hear a thing. Do you think that's what nineteen years of following Iron Maiden round the world has done to my hearing?' he said.

While the crowd behind him cheered on the Harlequins as they beat the Northampton Saints, John struggled to hear anything. 'What I can hear sounds alright,' he told me eventually.

As a young man he had followed the punk band The UK Subs. I once had some involvement with that band when working for their publishing company so I told him an anecdote. One evening after work, some 30 years before, I was confronted by three guys (one of them wielding a knife) in Oxford Circus underground station. They demanded money. I hardly had any, so I went through my pockets pleading poverty. After more threats, I found a pound note and reluctantly handed it over. 'Give us everything!' one of them demanded as another grabbed my arm. Then I noticed that one wore a UK Subs badge and I told them that I worked with the band. 'I was with them at the Top Of The Pops studio last week.'

'Brilliant,' said the guy with the knife, 'I saw that on TV. We love Charlie the singer.' At that moment the one who had taken my pound gave it back and said, 'Sorry about that, we'll get the next one.' He tried to give me a fifty pence piece as well, saying, 'If you are really short have this.' I declined and also suggested that mugging wasn't a great career option.

John listened to my story, then winked. 'Yep, that was probably me.'

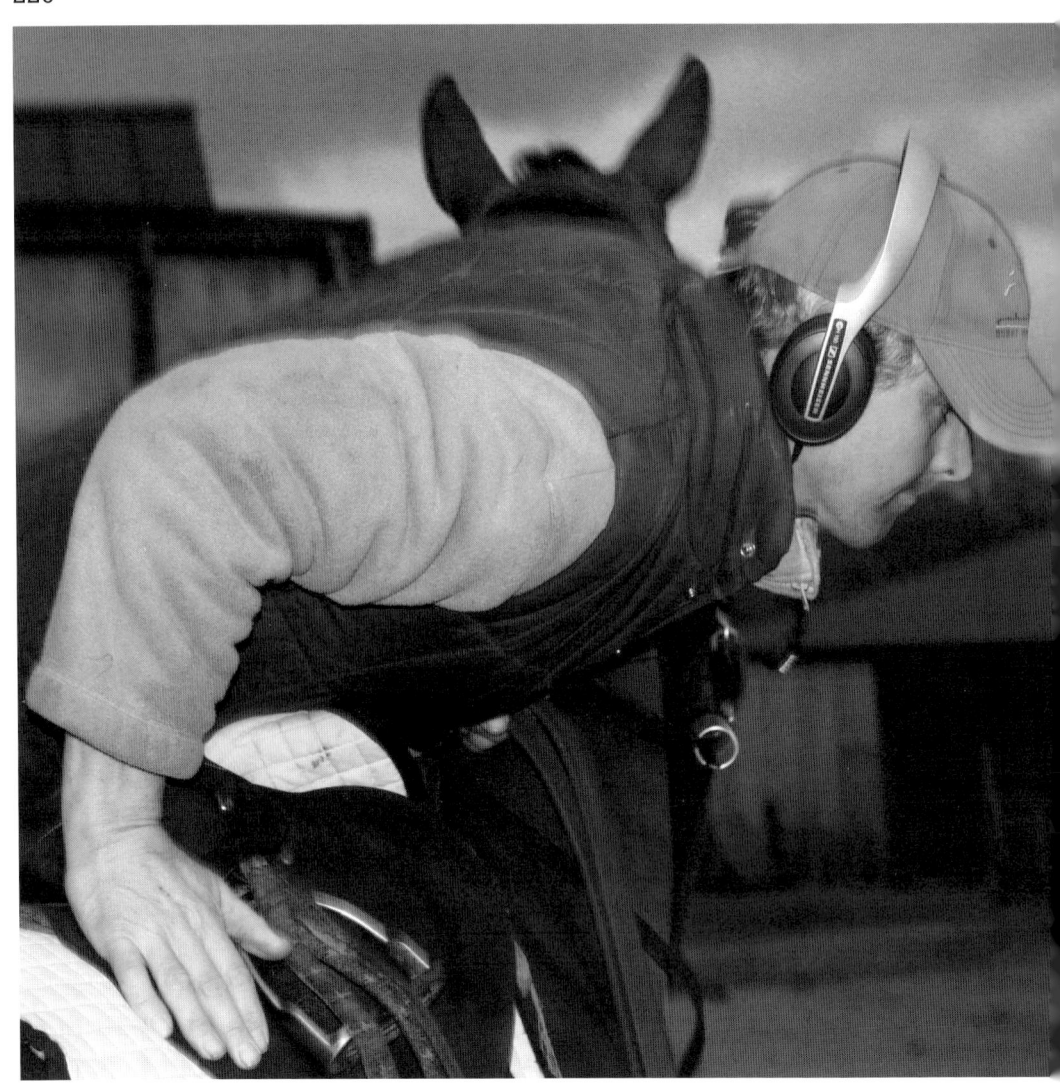

'It is not easy listening to music when riding.'

```
Name: Russell, horse breeder
Likes: The Kaiser Chiefs, Crosby, Stills and Nash
Familiar with Nick Drake's music: No
```

As Russell got on his horse Tilly in the evening gloom and started to canter around the manage next to his yard in Wales it became obvious that both were moving in time to Cello Song.

It was a real pleasure to watch and had I been a better photographer you would be able to see it too, but all I got was blurry images of the two of them cantering round. So you will have to make do with Russell mounting the horse. After they finished, he pointed out that horses will often fall into time with music but, as Tilly couldn't hear it, Russell had chosen the pace.

'It was surreal and disorientating riding around with headphones on,' he observed. He went on to say that he had been photographed before when his bottom had featured in an advert for Ladbrokes. He took the headphones off and handed them to me. 'It is very nice,' he said.
There is still some doubt in my mind as to whether he was talking about his bottom or the track.

'It's mind-blowing, innit? The arrangement is beautiful.'

In Oxford I came across Marcus, who was carrying a guitar case on his way to play. I had never heard of Marcus Bonfanti but two days later I found myself sixty miles away, in a pub in Notting Hill I had never been in before and noting that playing live on Sunday was one Marcus Bonfanti. I like a good coincidence but, of course, it would be a stranger world if there weren't coincidences.

Standing in one of the massive stone doorways in Christ Church, Marcus pulled on the headphones and listened. He closed his eyes, stood stock still, and looked like a man in heaven. As it finished, a huge smile lit up his face. 'That is truly beautiful and what a great setting to listen to it in. Can I keep it?'

As we chatted, Marcus opened his bag and generously gave me one of his CDs. This felt wrong so we argued a bit until he would allow me to pay for it. At home, I put it on. He has a heck of a bluesy sound and deserves much success.

The last thing Marcus said to me when we parted in Oxford was, 'Thank you, I feel quite privileged.'

What a nice guy. Go see him.

```
Name: Marcus, guitarist
Likes: old blues recordings, Robert Johnson,
       Howling Wolf, Mississippi John Hurt,
       Muddy Waters
Familiar with Nick Drake's music: Yes
```

'There is a purity about Kurt Kobain, Jeff Buckley and Nick Drake made even more poignant by their...um...deaditude.'

I had decided that one of the last pictures I would take would be of Nick Drake's biographer Trevor Dann. As I went to his London office, I spotted Julian Barratt of the Mighty Boosh sitting outside a café next door to Dann's office. He nodded at me with vague acknowledgement (I had photographed him a couple of months previously) but I could tell he didn't know why he knew my face.

I walked over and said, 'I'll give you a pound if you can remember why you know me. (I can be horribly annoying like that.)

'You're a writer,' he ventured.

'No,' I said, 'think Nick Drake.'

He turned to his companion and explained what I was doing. Julia, his partner and a huge Nick Drake fan, looked at him as if to say, and you never mentioned this? 'Can I hear it?' she asked.

I didn't want to refuse so we walked down the road away from the crowded café so she could put on the headphones.

As she was listening, a guy who was living rough on the streets, jumped over a fence and danced about, chatting with me while I took her photograph. Julia just smiled and continued to listen, aware of his presence but giving herself to the moment.

I loved how she boldly battled on after the phrase 'Made even more poignant by their…' when talking about the track. Faced with what seemed like a verbal cul-de-sac she invented the word 'deaditude' just to end it. Then she said, 'Oh no, I can't say that.' But it still makes me laugh every time I read it. Deaditude – the perfect ending.

```
Name: Julia, actor, writer
Likes: Free, heavy rock, Julian Cope
Familiar with Nick Drake's music: Very
```

'I was concentrating on it but I didn't get it at all.
It was very dirgy.'

As I am writing this Michael is about to release his first record. This CD will almost certainly go on to sell more copies than Nick Drake sold of all three of his albums together while he was alive. As one of the seven Chelsea Pensioners singing on the album Men In Scarlet, Michael has been incredibly busy with TV appearances and press junkets. I took this photograph during a break while he and the six other members of this veteran, uniformed version of Take That were recording a song for the Remembrance Day episode of Songs of Praise in a church in Folkestone. I have met Michael a few times as I had a tiny involvement with the album when it was recorded.

Actually, I twang a ruler like some over-enthusiastic schoolboy on a miked-up wooden desk on the first track of the album, a light-hearted version of the old army classic Bless 'Em All. Well, one has to be adaptable.

It does makes me think that I ought to turn up to future sessions not with a keyboard or a guitar but with a tiny flight-case full of differently sized rulers so that I can listen to a track, look at the producer, and say things like, 'Hmm, I think this calls for the twelve-inch metal' or 'This is a cheeky song. I suggest the six-inch see-through plastic ruler.'

Anyway, back to Michael, who I have to say hated the track with a vengeance proving two things: that 1) not everybody likes Nick Drake and 2) Michael is a very honest man.

```
Name: Michael, Chelsea pensioner
Likes: Mozart, Gilbert and Sullivan, easy listening
Familiar with Nick Drake's music: No
```

'There's a feeling of the music falling into the next phrase.'

```
Name: Miranda, dance student
Likes: Bonobo, Quantic Soul Orchestra,
     'anything with a good bass line'
Familiar with Nick Drake's music: Yes
```

Student dancer Miranda was sitting outside in the sun cooling down with a bottle of water. She had just come out of the studio where she had been doing a dance class and it turned out that she was a fan of Nick Drake's music.

She put the headphones on and listened, occasionally taking a sip of water. 'I've just been doing a release technique class,' she told me at the end, 'which is all about falling off-balance. The movements are fluid, as is this track. There's a feeling with this song of the music falling into the next phrase.' I thought this was a really interesting observation.

We shook hands and off I went…with moderate fluidity, I felt.

'The overall noise of it is just great.'

```
Name: Tony, motorcycle dealer
Likes: vocal harmony music , Woody Guthrie,
       Paul Brady, Margaret Barry. 'all sorts really'
Familiar with Nick Drake's music: Yes
```

Tony was possibly one of the biggest surprises in this whole project. I came across a motorcycle dealers called Tony Moss in Shropshire. It was raining and almost dark, but the light from within the shop indicated that it might still be open. I imagined I would go in and find someone who would not know Nick Drake's music at all.

When I opened the door a voice from the back called out and in the workshop behind the counter, I discovered Tony working on a bike. Spilling out over the many chromed machines around him was the sound of folk music – real English folk music. The Cuckoo by Cockersdale from the album Voices in Harmony greeted me. Yet again, I had to chastise myself for being judgmental: of course not all motorcycle shops vibrate to the sound of ZZ Top, Steppenwolf or Aerosmith.

It turned out that Tony was learning the banjo and regularly took part in folk evenings, jamming the night away at local hostelries. I loved watching him stamp his foot as he listened to the track, his hand keeping time on his thigh, while he hummed and sang in full voice.

'Great,' he said as he took the headphones off. 'I know that song. I loved its familiarity.'

I had walked in out of the rain and the dark into a warm haven that offered me tea and more surprises than I was about to offer the kind welcoming proprietor.

'Once you've dipped in to Nick Drake's music it just sticks.
 He is an extraordinary player
 – an amazing fucking player.'

```
Name: Martin, actor
Likes: The Beatles, Two Tone, Tamla Motown,
     Paul Weller, Fairport Convention
Familiar with Nick Drake's music: Very
```

Martin was very knowledgeable about Nick Drake and his music. He had recently been to see a Drake tribute act (Keith James) in Cardiff, which had re-invigorated his interest in the material. At first he was a little confused by what I was offering but once he had established that it was not a recording of me playing Cello Song he couldn't have been keener to listen, seeming more than happy to run a bit late for a meeting.

I knew that Martin had excellent musical knowledge because I'd heard him standing in on Danny Baker's radio show on Radio London a few times. He pointed out the differences in the recording and talked about how easy it was to forget how young both Drake and his arranger Robert Kirby were when they recorded Five Leaves Left.

'It was a little bit dry and cerebral.
It didn't make me cry but it took me far away.'

Name: Laura, tour guide
Likes: The Rolling Stones, The Arctic Monkeys
Familiar with Nick Drake's music: No

Canadian Laura has had the hots for Mick Jagger for ages and is a huge fan of the Stones.

I found her close to Hyde Park Corner when she was on a break from her job with one of the London tour bus companies.

She thought she detected an Indian influence to the track but also felt that there was a Celtic brogue to Drake's voice. Hearing it made her curious. Why, she speculated, would he take his own life and had he broken away from society, despite his middle class background? It takes a certain kind of person to be a tour guide, I thought. One who wants to get under the skin of other people. We laughed and discussed many things, and the second I said goodbye I missed her and her insightful questioning.

*'I feel bizarre – chilled yet hot.
Nick Drake is not natural squash music.'*

```
Name: Phil, charity director
Likes: Bob Marley, John Martyn
Familiar with Nick Drake's music: Very
```

I have known this man since I was in short trousers. Actually, this statement doesn't work very well in this context because I was wearing short trousers when I took the photograph.

On this particular day, I had manfully thrashed Phil on the squash court. I suggested he might like to put on the headphones before I thrashed him again. He readily agreed because he loves Nick Drake's music. But after he listened, he became an untouchable player, like a modern-day Jonah Barrington. It was like the old comic strip Billy's Boots from the comic Scorcher. In that young Billy Dane, a schoolboy and aspiring footballer, who was actually an extremely poor player, finds a pair of old-style, ankle-high football boots that had belonged to a famous professional footballer called Jimmy 'Dead Shot' Keen. Every time Billy put on the boots he played like a genius.

I knew Nick Drake was a fast runner and I wondered if he had been a particularly good squash player. Maybe that is what all sportsmen need: an injection of Nick Drake's music before getting into the blocks.

'The words are absolutely beautiful. He is like an angel singing.'

Janet held on tight to some iron work on the edge of a very foggy sea on the south coast of England. 'Gorgeous, absolutely gorgeous,' she said at the end of the track.

Janet's and my beliefs are worlds apart, but, at the same time, I would have bet my bottom dollar that something bizarre would happen while I was photographing her. And sure enough, after Janet had said, 'you know Nick Drake is with you and loves what you are doing' and 'he had a beautiful soul', in the far distance, a tall, thin young man appeared out of the fog, seemingly walking on the surface of the sea. When he got nearer, it became obvious that he was standing on a surf board with a paddle in his hands but for a moment I felt a tiny shiver down my spine.

I asked Janet if she could get in touch with Nick and she pointed out that 'it doesn't work like that', before continuing to talk about the track.

It was all lovely and interesting and then, as we parted, she looked into my eyes saying, 'remember who you are'. I was a tad disgruntled because this implied one of two things:

1) I had forgotten who I currently was.
or
2) There is more to me than I know about.

And I am afraid there isn't. Sorry…I am not afraid. There just isn't. Right?

Name: Janet, past life regression therapist
Likes: classical music especially Mozart and Chopin
Familiar with Nick Drake's music: No

*'It is like walking in a natural place
and occasionally you are surprised by say, an antelope.'*

```
Name: James, architectural engineer
Likes: Joni Mitchell, Nick Drake, Bowerbirds,
       Neil Young
Familiar with Nick Drake's music: Very
```

James said so many quotable things it was hard to know which one to put under this photograph. Here are a few more of his quotes for you.

'I felt quite emotional, but after the first 20 seconds it was fantastic.'

'It has a very English feel, but to have bongos over it gives it an interesting flavour, like a bit of spice to bangers and mash.'

'It's like that flurry of cellos is like a waterfall made of wood. They are really oaky.'

'It sends you into another mysterious world.'

And just to finish, my favourite, which made me want to cuddle him and stroke his beard.

'I am over the moon…the pink moon.'

'That's a smooth professional recording.'

Name: Don, decorator
Likes: Led Zeppelin
Familiar with Nick Drake's music: No

The snow was melting as I drove around looking for somewhere to stay in the Welsh hills. Without thinking, I went right to the end of a long drive and parked against a gate. I should have parked facing back outwards but, hey, I'm not that bright when it comes to parking cars and, after staying the night, in the morning my car had become bogged down in the newly revealed mud beneath the slush.

Heavy-Metal fan and all-round good guy Don came to my aid and placed some bits of carpet under my tyres. After that failed, we tried to tow it out with a car. Defeated again, he went and got a neighbour's tractor.

As Don went to remove the bits of carpet, I gave him the headphones. He said very little about the track but was amazed to hear that it was over forty years old. I think he was a little hacked off with me because he was now late for work and I had managed to cover him in mud when he had tried in vain to push the car back up the hill while I sat in the driving seat revving away, motionless in reverse gear. Oh, how we laughed…a few weeks later when I re-appeared with some chocolates and beer.

'Wow, fantastic. His voice is extraordinary.'

```
Name: Harry, actor
Likes: The xx, Neil Young, Local Natives,
       'I listen to everything'
Familiar with Nick Drake's music: Yes
```

Harry was on his way to grab a coffee so he could learn some lines when I asked if he was a Nick Drake fan. He was.

Harry, it turns out, has appeared in some of the biggest-grossing films of all times. But, he is unlikely to be recognised from them. The part he is best-known for nearly slipped through his hands towards the end of the series because he had lost five and a half stone. But a fat suit came to his rescue and he was able to reprise his role as the despicable, diet-shy Dudley Dursley in the final Harry Potter films.

Leaning against a railway bridge, Harry put the headphones on and the song started. Then something changed in his eyes. It was the look I had seen on the face of so many of the people I had stopped and grew to know as 'Strange Face' (the first two words of Cello Song's lyrics). The eyes start to lose focus as if indicating that the listener's thoughts are somewhere else.

Although more familiar with some of Drake's other work, Harry was really full of praise for the song. 'I love the humming.' he said 'His voice is just part of it. It could be on in the background, it doesn't overwhelm.'

'It's just the kind of rhythm to it made it feel like a walking song,' he continued. Eventually I left him to get on with learning his lines. I was tempted to put the headphones on myself to test out his walking theory. But I didn't.

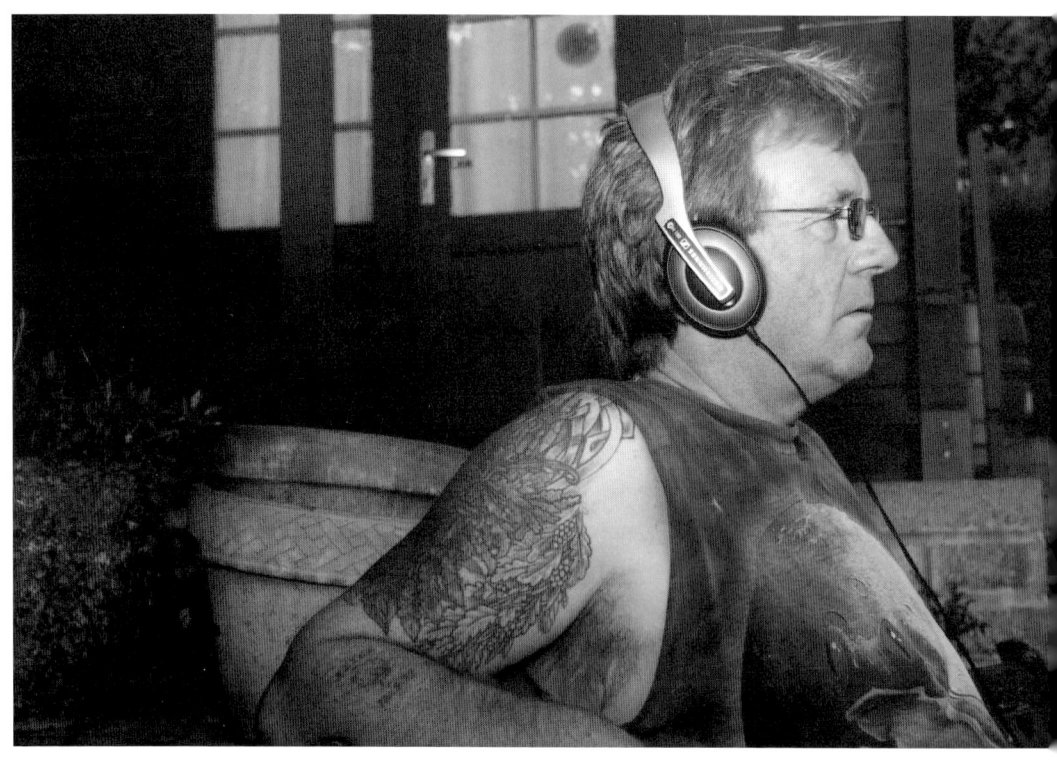

'That is not a bad starting point.
A recording that most Nick Drake fans haven't heard.'

```
Name: Alun, proprietor of a vegetarian
      bed-and-breakfast establishment
Likes: Coope, Boyes and Simpson, Brian Eno, punk,
      reggae, The Stranglers (original line-up),
      John Martyn, male voice choirs
Familiar with Nick Drake's music: No
```

In South Wales, Alun put on the headphones and listened. Not for the first time, I was surprised that someone who was a huge John Martyn fan was not aware of Nick Drake and, for that reason, I suspected that Alun was in for a treat. I wasn't disappointed and neither was he. When he removed the headphones, he smiled, 'That is so John Martyn-like. A little more complicated in the fingerwork. Man, that is so nice.'

After I told him about John Martyn and Nick Drake's friendship and Martyn's admiration of Drake's playing, he continued: 'It was great and something I would like to hear a lot more of. John Martyn was right calling him The Guv'nor. It makes me want to hear more Nick Drake.'

Then it was my turn to learn something. Alun, it turns out, is a druid. He is not allied to a particular 'grove' or order of druids but prefers to do his own thing. And for that reason Alun is known as a 'hedge druid'. I love that fact. I saw photographs of his wedding ceremony and it looked brilliantly earthy, beautiful, green and calm. I think I want to be a hedge druid now. I don't know what it entails but I just love the fact that I now know one and that I introduced him to Nick Drake. And he, in turn, introduced me to hedge druidity.

'You have made my day.'

```
Name: Ella, student violinist
Likes: The National
Familiar with Nick Drake's music: Very
```

I approached Ella primarily because she had a violin on her back. She was understandably reluctant to be photographed because taking off her helmet for the headphones, would reveal the ghastly phenomenon that is known as 'hat hair'. Instead she asked if she could just listen to the track. Sadly for her, the deal for this project was to listen and be photographed. I felt bad, especially as she loves Nick Drake's music, but rules is rules. We said goodbye and off she cycled.

Standing outside London's Royal Albert Hall wondering where my journey would take me next, I watched as she cycled into the distance. But after she had gone about two hundred yards she turned around and pedalled back. 'I can't bear not to hear it,' she said. With that, she took off her cycling helmet and out came her hair looking fine. She listened intently and afterwards agreed with me that it sounded like the same cellist multi-tracked on the performance. I was glad when she said that I had made her day. She had certainly made mine by returning and not being disappointed.

'Haunting.'

Name: Andrew, pianist, composer
Likes: Radio 3, Regina Spektor
Familiar with Nick Drake's music: No

This photograph was taken during the interval of a recital in a magnificent venue in Herefordshire next to the historic house Hellens. Andrew was the pianist but couldn't wait to hear how his beloved Aston Villa were doing in the quarter finals of the FA Cup. At this point (half time for both the recital and the match) Villa were two goals to nil down to Reading, news Andrew relayed to me, having heard it via a small radio he had brought with him.

Having put on the headphones, he walked about the beautiful grounds smoking, while I followed. He liked the track but when he took the headphones off he would only say one word – 'haunting' – about the recording, however much I encouraged him to say more.

Oh, and I know you want to know…Aston Villa eventually won the quarter-final four two, but were knocked out of the Cup in the semi-final by an in-form Chelsea side three goals to nil, although the then Villa manager, Martin O'Neill, accused referee Howard Webb of bottling it when he waved away a first-half penalty claim when John Obi Mikel blatantly brought down Gabriel Agbonlahor with a desperate last-man lunge, which O'Neill reasoned could have affected the outcome of the match.

I think.

'Have you heard this? This is really good.'

```
Name: Jeremy, broadcaster, writer
Likes: early Genesis (especially Selling England
     by the Pound)
Familiar with Nick Drake's music: No
```

Jeremy had not heard of Nick Drake, but when he told me that his favourite album was Selling England by the Pound I knew that he could only find a Nick Drake track a positive experience (obviously this doesn't necessarily follow but they were contemporaneous, so there was a good chance).

In an effort to describe how Nick Drake fitted into the world, I explained that he was regarded as a rather melancholy songwriter, who was a stablemate and friend of John Martyn. 'John Martyn?' Jeremy replied. 'Was he the one who sang like this?' He said the last two words in what can only be described as John Martyn styli: very slowly, deeply and muffled. 'That's him,' I said, smiling.

I showed him some of the photographs I had taken with people wearing headphones and he looked at one of Noel Fielding and exclaimed, 'He looks like Jesus!'

As the track started, Jeremy lit up a Marlboro, then glanced across and said loudly to his colleague, 'Have you heard this? This is really good.'

'That's actually really bloody good,' he told me at the end. 'He sounds like someone. It's not Barclay James Harvest, is it?'

A small boy approached, accompanied by his mother. 'He absolutely loves you and your show,' she said, and I watched as Jeremy was polite and considerate to a timid young autograph hunter. I shook his hand and left them to it.

'I am clearly going to spend the evening listening to Five Leaves Left.'

```
Name: Katie, student
Likes: Nick Drake, Elliot Smith, musicals,
       Alabama 3, Martin Simpson
Familiar with Nick Drake's music: Very
```

I needed some new guitar strings and was served by Katie, a keen Nick Drake fan.

Very few of the pictures I took show the listener engaging with the camera but Katie was an exception. Her demeanour changed between the beginning and end of the track. 'That,' she said, 'was incredibly soothing. I've had a horrible day at work and you have just made it great.'

'How astonishing. You don't often hear anything new as a biographer.
It sounds as though George Martin has popped into the studio.
Those cellos sound like they could have come from Sergeant Pepper.'

```
Name: Trevor, radio producer, broadcaster and
      Nick Drake biographer
Likes: Nick Drake, Frank Zappa, Lyle Lovett
Familiar with Nick Drake's music: Very
```

I had always wanted this to be the last picture I took for this book. Trevor Dann has loved Nick Drake's music since 1969 when he bought Five Leaves Left at a reduced price from a record shop. He adored it straightaway and told a friend at the time that he thought he had bought the greatest album ever. If there had been other people following Trevor Dann's lead back then, we may have heard a lot more material from Nick Drake.

Trevor's favourite track on Five Leaves Left is Cello Song. I knew that he wouldn't know of the existence of this alternative version so I went and knocked on his office door a couple of times to try to catch him unaware in order to be able to photograph the look of astonishment on his face when he heard it. This didn't happen, though, as he was never bloody in. So in the end I emailed him and he got in touch with me almost immediately. I got in the car, found a beautiful church (All Saints in Margaret Street) barely three hundred yards from Trevor's office, popped in and asked for permission from Dennis the administrator to take photographs in the courtyard then went and got Trevor.

We walked along the street back to All Saints and he told me that, despite having worked in the area for over twenty five years, he had never noticed the church.

As I looked at him through the camera I thought about what must be going through his head as he listened. Four years of research for his book about Drake, Darker Than The Deepest Sea, represents a lot of time, effort, care and consideration. The sleepless nights, the potential draining quality of being too close to Nick Drake and his music for too much time. I took my first edition copy of Trevor's biography in with me and asked him to sign it. 'Of course I will,' he said, 'although unsigned copies are rarer.'

I couldn't tell what he thought of my project, but at home, I opened the book and looked at the inscription: 'From a strange face, with regards Trevor.'

It made me smile.

Michael Burdett is a composer who, for the last twenty five years, has written theme and incidental music for television, radio, stage and film. He is the man behind the album Little Death Orchestra and still occasionally records under that name.

The Strange Face Project supports Nordoff Robbins, the UK's national music therapy charity.

www.nordoff-robbins.org.uk.

www.thestrangefaceproject.com

www.elastictv.com/elastictv/strangeface.html

www.littledeathorchestra.com

Acknowledgements

I would like to thank the following for their help and encouragement with The Strange Face Project, Claire Harcup, Sahar Shaker, Richard Burdett, Anne Burdett, Joe Boyd, Liz Roberts, Hector Proud, Eloise Rowley, Rosie Allerhand, Rachel Wood, Charlotte Sluter, Caroline Barby, James Townsend, Andi Campbell-Waite, Helga Berry, Clare Morris, Jon Grainger, David Wolff, John Wood, Jason Creed, Jon Henley, Nick Reeves, Tom Gibson, Richard Kennard, Roy Daintith, Nigel Mitchell, Kathryn Lacey, Sally Roberts, Murray Roberts, Sara Thompson, Gary Bryan, Rachel Walker and all at Nordoff Robbins. Thank you, thank you, thank you.